Rule Breaking and Political Imagination

Rule Breaking and Political Imagination

KENNETH A. SHEPSLE

The University of Chicago Press

Chicago and London

The University of Chicago Press, Chicago 60637
The University of Chicago Press, Ltd., London
© 2017 by The University of Chicago

Published 2017

26 25 24 23 22 21 20 19 18 17   1 2 3 4 5

ISBN-13: 978-0-226-47318-5 (cloth)
ISBN-13: 978-0-226-47321-5 (paper)
ISBN-13: 978-0-226-47335-2 (e-book)
DOI: 10.7208/chicago/9780226473352.001.0001

Library of Congress Cataloging-in-Publication Data

Names: Shepsle, Kenneth A., author.
Title: Rule breaking and political imagination /
Kenneth A. Shepsle.
Description: Chicago ; London : The University
of Chicago Press, 2017. | Includes bibliographical
references and index.
Identifiers: LCCN 2016055629 |
ISBN 9780226473185 (cloth : alk. paper) |
ISBN 9780226473215 (pbk. : alk. paper) |
ISBN 9780226473352 (e-book)
Subjects: LCSH: Political science. | Rules
(Philosophy)—Political aspects. | Parliamentary
practice. | Filibusters (Political science) | Politics,
Practical.
Classification: LCC JA71.S436 2017 | DDC 320.01—
dc23 LC record available at https://lccn.loc.gov
/2016055629

For the generation after next:
Zora, Rosy, and Gavin

"Know the rules well so you can break them effectively."
DALAI LAMA

"What's a constitution among friends?"
BOSS PLUNKITT
OF TAMMANY HALL

Contents

Acknowledgments

The present volume constitutes something of a departure for me—a collection of brief illustrative essays on the subjects of rule breaking and strategic imagination. I have collected these stories over many years but mainly while on the faculty of the Department of Government at Harvard University for thirty years, a frequent visitor at the Hoover Institution of Stanford University, and as the Tommaso Padoa-Schioppa Visiting Professor in the Department of Public Management of Bocconi University in Milan, Italy, during the 2013–14 academic year. I am very grateful to these three institutions for their hospitality and support. A fourth institution that provided for a decade, and continues to provide, extraordinary intellectual stimulation is the Program on Institutions, Organizations, and Growth of the Canadian Institute for Advanced Research (CIFAR). I am also grateful to audiences at Harvard Law School, Bocconi (Milan), Juan March Institute (Madrid), University of Milan, University of Mannheim, Hertie School (Berlin), Kellogg School (Northwestern University), Washington University (St. Louis), University of Warwick (Coventry, UK), London School of Economics, Trento Festival of Economics, CIDE (Mexico City), Brookings Institution (Washington, DC), and the meetings of the Midwest Political Science Association for listening to some of my ideas.

I acknowledge many individuals who have contributed to my thinking about rule breaking and imagination, including John Aldrich, Stephen Ansolabehere, Torun Dewan, Morris Fiorina, Andrew Hall, Gregory Koger, David Mayhew, Maxwell Palmer, Andrew Ruttan, Matthew Stephenson, and Adrian Vermuele. I also acknowledge the profound influence of my mentor, teacher, and friend, the late William H. Riker, whose blend of history writing, storytelling, and analytical thinking has served as a model for this book in particular but more generally as an approach to scholarship I have always found attractive. I am especially grateful to Lee Alston and Barry Weingast for their careful reading of an earlier draft of this book and for their forthright, constructive criticisms and suggestions that have heavily influenced the final result. Finally, there is the unpayable debt of a half century of love, support, and commitment from my wife, Rise. Neither she nor any of the other people or places named above is responsible for the use I have made of their generosity.

Kenneth A. Shepsle
Cambridge, MA

What's This Book About?

This is a book of stories about institutions and how they sometimes fail to perform in ways we expect. Institutions have figured prominently in theories of politics of the last half century. But it wasn't always this way. Although qualitative political science in the first part of the twentieth century put a premium on the role and importance of institutions, World War II and its aftermath pushed institutional analysis to the sidelines. The behavioral revolution, with its emphasis on the measurement of individual attitudes and behavior, arose from the confluence of social psychology and novel quantitative methodologies, especially scaling and survey research. Stouffer's classic, *The American Soldier* (1949), pioneered this approach. Individuals were the units of analysis, sometimes in isolation and other times embedded in a social or historical context.

Adapting these new methods to political topics, voting behavior and public opinion in particular, the behavioral revolution flourished as political scientists got better and better at measuring things about individuals and their environment. Modern political science was born in these years, but there was a growing sense that something was missing, that the behavioral revolution had wiped too much of the slate clean. For one thing, behaviorists provided few unifying principles for their descriptions, measurements, and hypotheses. Partially as a reaction to this theoretical vacuum, some postwar scholars in political science and economics began a new project—formal political theory (also called "rational choice theory," "positive political theory," "public choice," and sometimes even the old and oft-used label "political economy"). Individuals remained the units of analysis in these inquiries, but there was little emphasis on their accurate portrayal; rather, they were conceived of sparsely in terms of their *preferences* over potential political outcomes and their *beliefs* about how outcomes are produced as the resultant of individual *actions* (i.e., "how the world works"). Preferences, beliefs, and actions—mere shadows of real individuals—served as theoretical instruments to derive and explain *equilibrium patterns* at the group or societal level. Thus, to cite five influential exemplars, Downs (1957) proceeded in this manner to explicate voting and party competition in elections; Riker (1962) to characterize winning and losing coalitions in settings of interpersonal conflict; Schelling (1960) to produce insights about mixed-motive situations consisting of both conflict and cooperation; Olson (1965) to explain success and failure in collective action; and Buchanan and Tullock (1962) to portray the consequences of different constitutional arrangements. Politics, in this view, came to be understood as the result of instrumental behavior in which rational individuals transformed their preferences and beliefs into optimal actions that, in turn, combined into aggregate empirical patterns. Formal theory became a tool for deriving expectations that could be examined empirically. It provided an explanatory narrative that had been missing in behavioral scholarship.

Formal political theory shifted attention away from individual behavior per se (something that animated the research agenda of the behavioral revolution owing to its roots in social psychology). Instead it provided a stripped-down, optimizing model of man (Simon 1957) that yielded implications about *groups of individuals* in social, economic, and political settings. There was real value added in the form of analytical rigor. But still, there was something missing.

Institutions, that old chestnut of the late nineteenth and early twentieth centuries, were at best deep in the background and at worst ignored altogether by the more modern political science approaches, both behavioral and rational. As a formal modeler myself, but one also intrigued by the history and politics of the US Congress, I was struck by the schizophrenia many of my generation felt in our youth—modelers and methodologists by day but qualitative scholars of substance and history by night. In 1976, at a formal theory conference, it all came to a head for me when a prominent economist dismissed the richness of legislative politics with the observation that we didn't need much history or description once armed with the median voter theorem and other principles in the formal theory tool kit. For sure, I was pleased to claim credit with my formal theory colleagues for striking out in a productive new direction, but I was not ready to succumb to radical reductionism. This occasion began a personal intellectual odyssey for me (though I was not aware of this at the time) as I sought to bridge the chasm between the spare assumptions of rational choice theory and the rich substance of legislative institutions and practices.

I wrote a number of papers over the next decade (Shepsle 1979 and 1986 are illustrative) and participated in a fruitful collaboration with Barry Weingast (e.g., Shepsle and Weingast 1981, 1984, 1987), resulting in nearly a dozen papers during the 1980s incorporating and making salient the rules and practices of American legislatures. (In the 1990s, in collaboration with Michael Laver, I extended the scope of these arguments to parliamentary institutions; see Laver and Shepsle 1996.) This work put a premium on the structure of politics, made concrete by institutional arrangements and practices, within which individual preferences, beliefs, and actions take on meaning. I referred to the equilibrium patterns identified by this approach as *structure-induced equilibrium*. At about the same time, the classic statement of what came to be known as *the new institutionalism* was articulated by the late

Nobel laureate Douglass North, summarizing the realization that institutions structure and constrain rational action. An institution for North (1990, 3) consists of "the rules of the game in a society or, more formally, . . . the humanly devised constraints that shape human interaction." As the economic historian Joel Mokyr (2014, 152) observed, "North . . . stressed that institutions are essentially incentives and constraints that society puts upon individual behavior. Institutions are in a way much like prices in a competitive market: individuals can respond to them differently, but they must take them parametrically and cannot change them."

In the last quarter of a century, institutions have moved front and center as objects of analysis, returning from the exile imposed on them during the behavioral revolution. Not only are institutions conceived of as providing contexts for individual behavior but also as elements of choice themselves (Calvert 1993, 1995a, 1995b; Greif 2006; Schotter 1981). They may be seen as endogenous creations as well as exogenous constraints.* This latter development is significant. Groups of individuals—legislators, bureaucrats, voters, candidates, or parties—not only respond to institutional constraints according to this view, but they may also be in a position to alter these self-same constraints. Indeed, many institutions possess explicit self-altering features—methods to suspend, amend, or revise the very constraints according to which normal business is conducted.

North's new institutionalism and my structure-induced equilibrium take institutional rules as exogenously given. The Schotter-Calvert-Greif treatment of rules, on the other hand, allows institutional practices to emerge and to change as matters of collective choice. In both of these approaches, the rules, whether

---

*As Rowe (1989, viii) puts it, "Though institutional constraints could be imposed on human behavior just like the physical constraints imposed by natural resources and technology, such a fiction could not explain the institutional constraints themselves."

imposed or chosen, whether fixed or mutable, are understood to channel the choices of individual actors.

But what if they do not? An attempt to answer this question is what this book is about. The essays to follow illustrate how the scope for action is enlarged, despite the nominal constraining effects of rules, by *imagination* and by *transgression*. Imagination may be thought of as a "work-around." It is a resourceful tactic to "undo" a rule by creating a path around it without necessarily defying it—figuring out a novel way to untie the Gordian knot as it were. Imagination is vision and revision. As McLean (2001, 231) describes it in terms of admiration for former British prime minister Lloyd George, "Once in a while there comes a politician who sees further than the others. Such a politician can see opportunities where others do not." Transgression, on the other hand, is rule breaking; it is cheating; it is *cutting* the Gordian knot. There is no pretense of reinterpretation; it is defiance pure and simple. Whether imagination or disobedience is the source, constraints need not constrain, ties need not bind. This is what I hope to convince the reader of by arguments and examples.

Allowing for imaginative reinterpretation or outright violation forces a reconsideration of institutions as "humanly devised constraints." They structure the proceedings of a group or society—and thus are part of equilibrium patterns—only insofar as their rules are obeyed by most in the group most of the time. They are something else when observance is problematical or discretionary—when a rule operates more as a suggestion than a constraint. Put differently, what humans devise, they may revise or defy.* Illustrating these possibilities with select examples is my remit in this volume.

---

*Harstad and Svensson (2011) make this same point in distinguishing *lobbying* (revising) and *bribing* (defying). Bates (2014, 57) offers a time-scale interpretation: rule breaking is a short-run departure from institutional practice, whereas rule change derives from longer-term considerations.

The essays of this book do not provide a theory of imagination or rule breaking. What they provide are instances of the two, instances that I believe will impress and entertain the reader and, most importantly, caution him or her against unreflective thinking about the controlling authority of institutions. The essays are what one reviewer called "a meditation on institutions," neither systematic empirical analysis nor rigorous formal theory but rather a midcourse pause for reflection. As a project, the essays here comprise a genre shared by the stories in William Riker's (1986) *The Art of Political Manipulation* and Iain McLean's (2001) *Rational Choice and British Politics*. I hope the reader finds them as compelling.*

The remainder of part I elaborates institutions as rules, and imagination and rule breaking as forms of liberation from their constraints. Part II focuses on instances of imagination and rule breaking, with special attention to (and admiration for) the politicians who imaginatively exploit the situations in which they find themselves by novel stratagems or simply by breaking the rules. The essays mainly focus on legislative and electoral settings. Part III expands the scope to other institutional settings. I conclude by asking "So what?"

By the end, some readers may feel prepared to conclude that institutions do not constrain at all—that life is rife with rule breaking, illegality, and corruption. In talks I gave in Italy and Mexico, audience members suggested as much, claiming that in their countries, rule following, not rule breaking, was the exception. I think this goes too far. My simple claim is that institutions do create channels through which behavior flows, but occasionally the banks defining the channels are breached.

---

*There is a large analytical literature in political science and economics on institutions, some of which is listed in the references at the end of this volume. I have not made this body of work the focus here and have mainly relegated analytical matters to footnotes for the interested reader.

Part I
Basic Ideas

· 1 ·

Rule Breaking

Introduction

Imagine we are on Capitol Hill in early January of an odd-numbered year. Congress is about to convene, the even-year election having been decided the previous November. But is it a *new* Congress? As we will see, this is a constitutionally controversial matter, one that lies at the heart of more abstract matters concerning the nature of institutions of self-governing groups.

For the House of Representatives, this is a settled matter. The previous House had adjourned sine die before the election and, from a constitutional perspective, is now an entirely new body. The newly convened House will operate under "general parliamentary law" until it has sworn in its members, elected a presiding officer, and adopted standing rules.

For the Senate, on the other hand, this is *not* a settled matter. For two-thirds of the senators, the election of the previous November in no way interrupted their respective careers. They are sitting senators who were not "in cycle" for the election—their staggered terms did not require them to face contract renewal in the just-concluded election. Under one constitutional view,

This is a revised and shortened version of "The Rules of the Game: What Rules? Which Game?," chapter 5 in *Institutions, Property Rights and Economic Growth: The Legacy of Douglass North* © Cambridge University Press 2014. Reprinted with permission. See Shepsle (2014).

this Senate is the same collective body as the one that existed before the election; it never adjourned permanently (it *recessed*), and only a portion of its membership may have changed. More generally, the Senate of time t is the same as the one of time $t - 1$. By induction, a current Senate is the same body as the one that convened on March 4, 1789! There is never a new Senate. This is the *continuing-body* theory of the Senate (Bruhl 2010).

The continuing-body theory has interpretive consequences for rules that follow from several constitutional and statutory provisions. The first is Article I, Section 5 of the Constitution. This reads in part: "Each House may determine the Rules of its Proceedings. . . ." That is, each chamber is a self-governing group. The Constitution is otherwise modest in restricting internal features of each chamber.*

The second provision is a standing rule, authorized by the Article I, Section 5 rule-making requirement. Rule V of *The Standing Rules of the Senate* states:

1. No motion to suspend, modify, or amend any rule, or any part thereof, shall be in order, except on one day's notice in writing, specifying precisely the rule or parts proposed to be suspended, modified, or amended, and the purpose thereof. Any rule may be suspended without notice by the unanimous consent of the Senate, except as otherwise provided by the rules.

---

* Article I, Section 5 lays out a short list of requirements. Each chamber is the judge of elections to it; a majority constitutes a quorum; it may compel attendance of its members and set penalties for violations; it may punish members for disorderly behavior; it may expel a member on a two-thirds vote; it must keep a journal of proceedings and publish it; and it may not adjourn for more than three days without the consent of the other chamber. In addition, Article I, Section 2 specifies that the House shall choose a speaker and other officers, while Article I, Section 3 designates the vice president of the United States as the president of the Senate and implores the Senate to choose other officers including a president pro tempore who presides in the absence of the vice president.

2. The rules of the Senate shall continue from one Congress to the next Congress unless they are changed as provided in these rules.

A third provision, also a standing rule of the Senate, prescribes how standing rules may be amended as permitted by Rule V. According to Rule XXII.2, if sixteen Senators sign a motion to bring debate on any measure to a close (*cloture*), then the presiding officer

> shall at once state the motion to the Senate, and one hour after the Senate meets on the following calendar day but one, he shall lay the motion before the Senate and direct that the clerk call the roll, and upon the ascertainment that a quorum is present, the Presiding Officer shall, without debate, submit to the Senate by a yea-and-nay vote the question: 'Is it the sense of the Senate that the debate shall be brought to a close?' And if that question shall be decided in the affirmative by three-fifths of the Senators duly chosen and sworn—*except on a measure or motion to amend the Senate rules, in which case the necessary affirmative vote shall be two-thirds of the Senators present and voting* [emphasis added]—then said measure, motion, or other matter pending before the Senate, or the unfinished business, shall be the unfinished business to the exclusion of all other business until disposed of.

As a self-governing group, in sum, the Senate may formulate its own rules of procedure as well as rules governing the revision of those rules (Article I, Section 5 of the Constitution). However, absent such rule-governed amendments to the rules (requiring majority support to pass but two-thirds support to close debate as specified in Rule XXII.2 of the Senate's standing rules), the rules of one Congress continue to the next (as specified in Rule V.2 of the standing rules).

Now imagine the following hypothetical exercise.* At the opening of a new Congress, the majority leader, who, according to Senate rules, possesses priority in recognition, rises in the well of the Senate and announces, "As the Senate is not a continuing body, its first order of business, under Article I, Section 5 of the Constitution, is to select standing rules for the new Congress in accord with general parliamentary procedure. I move the re-adoption of the standing rules of the previous Congress, with two exceptions. Rule V.2 is deleted. And the special treatment given to cloture as applied to amendments to standing rules in Rule XXII.2 [italicized in the previous paragraph] is removed."†

After this motion is read, chaos breaks out in the chamber. The presiding officer, the vice president, gavels the chamber to order and recognizes the minority leader who, with great agitation, seeks recognition. "I rise to make a point of order. The Senate *is* a continuing body and thus is governed by the rules today that were in effect in the last session, not by general parliamentary procedure. This is clearly stated in Rule V.2. Thus it is possible to revise the rules only in compliance with Rule XXII.2, even if the objective is to revise said rule." The key question to be ruled upon by the presiding officer is whether the previous Senate can bind its successor (as Rule V.2 would seem to do).

Because the majority leader has invoked a constitutional basis for moving to adopt rules, the presiding officer would normally yield to the norm of not ruling on a constitutional point him- or herself; instead he or she would entertain a motion to table the point, thus allowing the fate of the minority leader's intervention to be determined by the full Senate. If the motion to table succeeds (thus rejecting the minority leader's point of order), the majority leader's motion to adopt new rules then becomes the

---

*I thank David Rohde for first bringing this possibility to my attention and Gregory Koger for further discussion.

†The most important feature of general parliamentary procedure is that decisions are taken by a simple majority, subject to a quorum being present.

unfinished business before the Senate. If the motion to table fails, then the majority leader's motion is effectively off the agenda.

A second key question arises—if the motion to table succeeds, is the subsequent unfinished business (the majority leader's motion to adopt rules) to be debated under the old Senate rules or according to general parliamentary procedure? The presiding officer rules that if the point of order is tabled, the Senate will proceed immediately to the majority leader's motion under general parliamentary procedure. The minority leader then appeals the chair's ruling, arguing that it makes no sense to consider the majority leader's motion under general parliamentary procedure because this is precisely what the majority leader's rules-change motion aims to establish but has not yet done so; the motion thus must, in the humble opinion of the minority leader, be taken up under existing Senate rules. That is, the majority leader's motion is predicated on the Senate *not* being a continuing body but, in the minority leader's view, *until* that is established, the Senate must operate under the old rules, not general parliamentary procedure. When the appeal of the presiding officer's ruling is put to a vote, a majority votes to sustain the ruling. (Senate majorities rarely overturn rulings of the presiding officer.) The minority leader's objection is thus tabled, his or her appeal defeated, and the majority leader's motion is taken up under general parliamentary procedure. A simple majority then approves his or her motion. *Voilà!* A revision of the rules—in effect a reduction in the threshold to end filibusters on amending the rules from two-thirds to three-fifths—has been accomplished by a simple majority. Moreover, a precedent has been set that the Senate is not a continuing body.

This is just a story, one in which we have dived deeply into the weeds of Senate procedure. However, it illustrates several points that will be the focus of this essay:

- Self-governing groups create the rules that govern their proceedings.

- Self-governing groups may change their rules—suspend, amend, override, even disobey.
- Let me repeat this last point. Self-governing groups may even flout the rules to which they have previously agreed (as they did in regard to Rule V.2 in the illustration just given).

Two Views of Institutions*

Douglass North (1990, 3; see also Mantzavinos, North, and Shariq 2004) is famously associated with characterizing an institution as a *game form*.[†] To repeat his famous definition, an institution is "the rules of the game in a society or, more formally, . . . the humanly devised constraints that shape human interaction." North urges us to think flexibly about this definition. At one end of the continuum are informal constraints: taboos, customs, conventions, codes of behavior, and traditions. At the other end are formal rights, responsibilities, and constraints like those found in contracts, official procedures, and constitutions. An institution specifies the players whose behavior is bound by its rules; the actions the players must, may, must not, or may not take (Crawford and Ostrom 1995); the informational conditions under which they make choices; a script of their timing; the impact of exogenous events; and the outcomes that are a consequence of these choices and events. The game form is transformed into a game when players are endowed with, and thus motivated by, preferences over outcomes.

The *game-form view of institutions*, one to which I adhered in earlier work on the role of institutional structure on political outcomes (Shepsle 1979), is silent on three significant matters. First, this approach says little about the origins of institutions. Institutional arrangements are taken as exogenously given with

---

*This is more fully developed in Shepsle (2006 a, 2006b) and independently developed in Munger (2010).

[†]Also see Hurwicz (2008).

the objective of tracing the implications of these rules for behavior and outcomes. Attention is riveted on the subsequent play of the game governed by these rules and the outcomes that arise from this play, not on the origins of the rules.* Second, there is little consideration given to the durability of rules. Because they are taken as exogenous, they are not, themselves, part of the play of the game. They are assumed to endure. Third, the constraints entailed in the rules are regarded as self-enforcing. There simply is no provision made for deviating from the rules. An agent, at any node in the game tree to which he or she is assigned, has a fixed repertoire of alternative actions as specified by the branches emerging from the node, and must choose from among these.† It would never occur to a majority leader of the US Senate, staring into the mirror in the morning, to contemplate announcing, contra Rule V.2, that the Senate is not a continuing body. This is not an available option.

The *equilibrium view of institutions*—an alternative perspective associated with the work of Schotter (1981) and Calvert (1993, 1995a, 1995b)—does not focus primarily on institutional origins either, but it does have something to say about their durability and prospects for departures from their strictures. According to this approach, the game form itself is part of the equilibrium.‡

---

* For a general model of endogenous institutions, see Eguia and Shepsle (2015). Alston notes that in taking a long view, economic historians are able to observe both the determinants of institutions and their consequences. That is, they do not have to take institutions as fixed but rather as emergent and evolving. See Alston, Harris, and Mueller (2012).

† See the figure and discussion in chapter 2. As the late game theorist Nobelist Leonid Hurwicz (2008, 284) asserted, a game-form description makes sense only if "players will not or cannot cheat, that they will consider only strategies prescribed by the mechanism governing the system, what we call the 'legal' strategies."

‡ For a treatise, weaving together game theory and economic history to develop an elaborate theory of endogenous institutions, see Greif (2006). Greif is one of the exceptions in focusing on institutional origins as well as on equilibrium properties— at p. 137ff. and chapter 7. Greif's approach differs slightly from Calvert-Schotter, mainly at the level of nuance, so I will group the three together for present pur-

What North took as exogenous, Calvert, Schotter, and Greif view as the endogenous product of strategic action in a more primal environment. There are really two parts to equilibria of interest: the outcome induced by play under a particular body of rules (*institutional* or *structure-induced equilibrium*; Shepsle 1979)— this is the one on which North focuses—and the one arising in the primal environment where rules are chosen and maintained (*equilibrium institution*; Shepsle 1986). The combination of these two elements is what Calvert, Schotter, and Greif have in mind as an institution—it is "an equilibrium of behavior in an underlying game. . . . It must be rational for nearly every individual to almost always adhere to the behavioral prescriptions of the institution, given that nearly all other individuals are doing so" (Calvert 1995a, 58, 60). Or as Greif (2006, 136) observes, "institutionalized rules and the beliefs they help form enable, guide and motivate most individuals to adopt the behavior associated with their . . . position [in the game] most of the time."

This means that the rules themselves are part of the equilibrium. Perturbations in the primal environment may undermine the existing rules equilibrium in any of several ways. A shock may change individual preferences over institutional arrangements, thus diminishing support for the existing regime. Alternatively, a shock may alter beliefs about the faithfulness of others to existing rules, thus causing one to recalculate his or her best response to existing rules and practices. Finally, a shock may modify one's

---

poses. A close cousin of this approach is Krehbiel (1991), where he articulated the Majoritarian Principle, or "remote majoritarianism," according to which decisive coalitions always lurk in the background on matters of institutional choice and maintenance. In addition, there is a vast literature in political science and political economy that analyzes the emergence of institutions alongside a consideration of their operating characteristics. This includes, but is not limited to, the origins and influences of parties (Aldrich 1995, 2011; Cox and McCubbins 1993); the process of democratization (Acemoglu and Robinson 2006; Lizzeri and Persico 2004); the structure of executives (Gailmard and Patty 2013); and legislative-executive relations in parliamentary democracies (Cox 1987). I could list many more examples.

own beliefs about how the world works and thus one's willingness to go along with existing institutional practices or to defect instead. In any of these ways, opportunities and incentives to change the rules may arise. Consider an exogenous change in constituency preferences caused, say, by the bursting of a housing bubble, a technological development, hyperinflation, a natural resource discovery, a commodity price change, or an environmental disaster. This may change either the composition of legislators, or the preferences or beliefs of existing legislators, which, in turn, may provide the circumstance for changing institutional rules—say, the elimination of the filibuster in the Senate.

Many institutions provide explicit avenues for suspension or revision of existing rules. This has already been mentioned for the Senate—Rule XXII describes how the Senate may amend its standing rules. Moreover, the Senate allows for suspending any of its rules by unanimous consent. The House, on the other hand, devises routine procedural routes around its standing rules, either by a suspension-of-the-rules motion (requiring two-thirds support of those present and voting) or by the majority adoption of a special rule brought to the floor by the Committee on Rules. The former allows a move directly to a vote, while the latter replaces existing rules with a specially crafted procedure. In either case, the procedure applies provisionally to take up a specific measure after which existing rules are put back in play.

There is a second methodological possibility this broader view of institutions permits. The North view of institutions does not countenance departures from the rules. They are assumed to be obeyed, although this remains implicit. In the Calvert-Schotter-Greif formulation, on the other hand, deviation is entirely possible. The Senate majority leader *can* announce that the Senate is not a continuing body, even though Rule V.2 declares that it is (so long as a majority is prepared to support this departure). The Senate is a self-governing group and can depart from its rules as it wishes. The more comprehensive equilibrium view of institutions associated with the Calvert-Schotter-Greif approach does not *assume* that compliance with the rules necessarily occurs, and therefore allows for deviation.*

Endogenous Procedures to Change Rules

There are multiple mechanisms incorporated into the rules by which those rules may be changed. That some such mechanisms exist at all is partially due to the self-awareness of institutional designers at a constitutional moment that they are not omniscient. Mechanisms are provided ex ante to fill unanticipated gaps, to adapt to changing circumstances, and to deal with circumstances as they arise that could be imagined ex ante but are too unlikely or too convoluted to accommodate at the rules-selection stage.

One conspicuous instance of these is a constitutional clause that describes the method by which a constitution may be amended. This is the role played by Article V of the US Constitution. At the constitutional convention of 1787, many of its participants made clear that they sought a less-than-unanimous procedure, given the unanimity straitjacket into which the Articles of Confederation had placed the existing regime, but one that may not be exploited too easily.

Bodies of rules, likewise, often possess amendment procedures. Rule XXII of the Senate's standing rules is, as we have seen, one such instance. Suspension of the rules, special rules from the Committee on Rules, and motions to waive points of order (that would otherwise be in order) are examples drawn from the US House that temporarily eliminate a constraint on procedure. Other sources of institutional change include interpretive courts, escape clauses (in treaties and labor-market agreements), nulli-

---

*Thus, a body of rules—an institution or constitution—is in equilibrium if there is no incentive and means to violate or alter this body. As Levinson (2011, 745) observes, "In order for constitutions to serve as the rules of the political game, they must avoid *becoming* the political game" (emphasis in original).

fication arrangements, emergency powers (see Loveman [1993] on "regimes of exception" and Lintott [1999] on the "dictator" institution of the Roman Republic), devolution, redistricting, and expansion (contraction) of (s)electorates.

Without going into further detail about these rules-revision mechanisms, it should be clear that rules are provisional. They continuously face three strategic challenges: (1) At the level of individual behavior, is it in any agent's interest to deviate from behavior required or expected by the existing institutional arrangements? (2) At the collective level, are there the means and the will to enforce rules and punish violators? (3) Is it in the interest of a decisive coalition to violate or alter the rules? Rules may be altered provisionally (as in a motion to suspend the rules) or more permanently (Article V of the US Constitution); they may be altered in the primal environment (as happened to the Articles of Confederation and the French ancien régime); and they may be disobeyed (as we shall see).

Self-governing groups have a commitment problem. Rules may serve a variety of purposes and confer conspicuous advantages, but by its very nature, a self-governing group cannot commit to sticking to them. There is no bond to post, no hostage to give. Like the all-powerful Hobbesian sovereign, a self-governing group can break any promise it makes. Its members may *choose* to obey its rules and follow its procedures, but then again, they may choose otherwise in any particular situation. Lest one thinks this merely an abstract problem with no practical significance, the essays of parts II and III provide concrete illustrations of imaginative maneuvering around rules as well as outright violations.

Rule Breaking: Some Further Considerations

Violating a rule in a given instance is one thing, but formally changing a rule is another. A revised rule subjects all future considerations to the new constraint. However, legislators, lacking omniscience, may be uncertain what future considerations might fall within the purview of the new rule. Reducing the threshold for cloture in the Senate, for example, means that *any* measure subsequently taken up will have an easier route to a final-passage vote than under a more stringent threshold. Sometimes, senators are prepared to take this leap—the filibuster criterion was, in fact, changed in 1917, 1975, and 2013. But many attempts in the intervening years failed. Why? Perhaps because many senators anticipated they might actually benefit from a more stringent cloture threshold, not always but often enough and on issues of great enough significance to a senator compared to those on which he or she would be disadvantaged. Indeed, for this very reason, the imaginary scenario with which I introduced this essay—in which the Senate majority leader's strategic maneuver resulted in abolishing the super-majority requirement altogether—might not succeed. Many in the majority may be loath to participate in the majority leader's procedural ploy.

Pervasive uncertainty about the contents of the future domain of a revised rule is often sufficient to deter rules changes—better the devil you know, and all that. But it is not necessary. Even if legislators know that many, even most, will be beneficiaries of the change, if they are uncertain about the identity of beneficiaries, they may still balk at making changes—they wonder will they be among the many beneficiaries or not? Uncertainty about future incidence produces a *status quo bias* (Fernandez and Rodrik 1991). This status quo bias means that permitting the occasional, one-time-only "breach" or temporary "reinterpretation" of the rules may be superior to tampering with the rules directly. Thus, one problem of collective commitment to rules is a variant of *time inconsistency* in which the circumvention of a particular rule on a particular occasion is a temptation too attractive to resist at the time.

It is worth noting a second development. It is not unusual for majorities simultaneously to agree to standing rules ex ante, but also both to provide mechanisms for temporary suspension and to leave loopholes that may be exploited in particular circumstances. The provision of these mechanisms and loopholes, and their anticipated use from time to time, identifies how the collectivity envisages the occasional circumvention. However, toleration for actually *breaking* rules is a horse of an altogether different color. That is, arranging a procedure for suspending rules in a particular circumstance and providing some regulation of its use (e.g., a super-majority requirement) is one thing. But permitting a simple majority to accept an outright violation damages the rules-as-constraints vision of institutions.

Conclusion

The institutions-as-constraints approach has been a workhorse in the positive political theory and political economy fields—Baron-Ferejohn bargaining games, Shepsle-Weingast amendment games, Romer-Rosenthal agenda games are examples. Collective practices are taken as fixed exogenously, providing a strategic context in which agents interact. In taking practices as fixed, equilibrium is established in which deviations from the game form are ignored (or repressed) and compliance is taken for granted. The game form is given ex ante, and there is no choice on whether to play it as opposed to some alternative game form.

The idea of institutions as constraints on behavior is a necessary, though incomplete, approach. It allows for an understanding of how collective activity proceeds when most people obey the rules. However, the institutions-as-equilibria approach allows a deeper appreciation of institutional life by taking on board the possibility that departures from the rules are possible. A self-governing group, like the Hobbesian state, cannot commit to enforcing its rules always and everywhere; thus, individual agents may find circumstances in which it does not always pay to comply with existing rules. Prospective departures, however, are not all of the same type. I have identified four different senses in which departures from a given body of rules are possible.

First, an institution is, as Calvert and Schotter remind us, embedded in a primal environment. If the institution is initially in equilibrium, then an environmental perturbation may be sufficient to provide incentives for agents to "move against" the institution. A regime in place may be replaced by an alternative arrangement, peacefully (e.g., the Articles of Confederation regime) or violently (e.g., the ancien régime in France).*

Second, a body of rules may contain its own mechanisms for revision. Article V of the US Constitution and Rule XXII of the Senate's standing rules are examples. Rules governing redistricting and reapportionment might also be regarded as self-referential mechanisms of planned adjustment to changes in the primal environment. Unlike departures of the first type (in the previous paragraph), where the impetus for departure from the rules comes in the form of unexpected changes in the primal environment, mechanisms of change here are prearranged by forward-thinking designers at a constitutional moment.

Third, rules may be temporarily suspended in accord with institutionally specified regulations. Suspension and special rules in the House, unanimous consent agreements in the Senate, escape clauses in treaties and contracts, and emergency powers in constitutions are examples. They share in common the belief that once the issue at hand is resolved, a return to "normal order" is expected.

Finally, rules may be broken. Declaring the Senate not a continuing body in direct contradiction of a standing rule clearly flouts the rules in place. A collectivity may have the means to re-

---

*The analogy to Schumpeterian "creative destruction" is suggestive, although for Schumpeter, a new regime or product or firm constitutes an improvement over its predecessor. I am not convinced by this teleology: one regime is superior to its predecessor by the lights of a decisive agent or coalition, but whether this is more broadly welfare improving is debatable.

verse outcomes based on rules violations or to punish deviations, but it may lack the will to do so.

All of these departures from rules raise concerns with the institutions-as-constraints approach. Institutions may, as North states, consist of "humanly devised constraints." But what humans devise, they can violate or revise. Thus, institutions are constraints except when decisive coalitions decide they are not. The examples given in essays to follow suggest that clever institutional politicians are on the prowl for opportunities to bend, evade, and even break the rules.

A second concern revolves around the difference between revising rules and breaking them. Revising is forever (or at least until the next round of revision). Breaking is issue- and time-specific. The policeman looks the other way when a motorist travels forty miles per hour in a thirty-five-miles-per-hour zone; he neither enforces the rule nor attempts to have it revised but rather allows the breach to stand. Likewise, legislative majorities often ignore small procedural violations, indeed sometimes even providing blanket waivers of points of order against these violations. Small departures, some of the time, appear to keep an institution intact. It endures occasional violations and defies revision.

What we observe in many empirical settings is neither rigid adherence to rules nor the complete abandonment of rule-based discipline. The primal environment suffers the "slings and arrows of outrageous fortune" and institutional actors respond, sometimes adhering to, sometimes revising, and other times violating institutional rules. Whether adherence, revision, or violation is the more common response to shocks, the main message in the essays to follow is that entrepreneurial politicians will always seek to do better, by hook or by crook.

· 2 ·

Imagination

In the previous essay, I examined rule breaking as a path of escape from the strictures of rule-based order. In the present essay, I explore an alternative route around the rules—imaginative stratagems.

Imagination is a difficult concept to wrap one's mind around. Its exercise is revealed in actions that are unexpected and novel. An imaginative move is often admired for its cleverness (even if not always for its effect). It is the product of vision, of seeing an unconventional way forward or a solution that had escaped previous notice. When observed by others, it frequently elicits a slap on the forehead and a "why didn't I think of that?" response. In a number of the essays in part II, we will encounter politicians who have reputations for the unexpected, the novel, the clever—in short, for seeing solutions others have overlooked.

We can conceptualize imagination in terms of a game of strategy. In its extensive form, a game is represented by a connected set of nodes and branches—a game tree. Each node names the agent who may act if the path of action should reach it. The branches emanating from a node are the choices or actions the named individual may take. Each choice leads to a new node with a newly named player and the set of alternative actions he or she make take. Once a choice is made, the path of the game is limited to a restricted set of possibilities (a subgame), namely

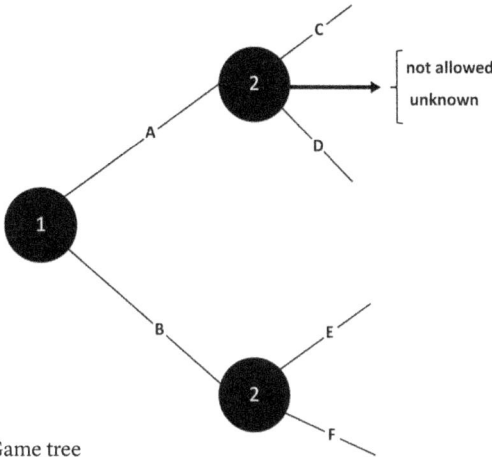

Figure 2.1: Game tree

only the paths that follow the branch that has been chosen; an entire set of nodes, branches, and paths are eliminated once a choice at a given node is made.

In figure 2.1, the first individual chooses between A and B. In either case, the second individual chooses next. If 1 chose B, then 2 chooses between E and F. If 1 chose A, then 2 chooses between C and D. But exercising his or her imagination, 2 sees a third way (the branch given by the darker arrow). It is unknown to 1 and may even be against the rules.

The game terminates in an outcome which assigns payoffs to each of the agents. In most applications (putting the thick branch to one side for the moment), this game tree is assumed to be commonly known to its players, and the players are assumed to be fully rational in making their choices when called upon to do so. We may think of the commonly known nodes, branches, and assigned players as the *rules of the game,* North's (1990) definition of an institution.*

If everything is commonly known about a game among its

---

*I have simplified the description of a game, but the features are described sufficiently for me to discuss imagination.

fully rational players—information is complete—then it is hard to see how imagination can figure in its play. At any node, the fully rational named player can determine how best to choose an alternative branch by thinking ahead to how other fully rational players will play at subsequent nodes that are reached.* Thus, any player can figure out the entire path of play and nothing is left to imagination. This is obvious in a simple game of strategy, like tic-tac-toe, where the first named player optimally chooses the center cell of a three-by-three grid and play proceeds from there, always ending in a draw if each player makes his or her best choice at subsequent stages. But what about a variation on the game: a five-by-five grid in which a winner is the first to get three Xs or Os in a row, or more generally an n-by-n grid where a winner is the first to get k of her marks in a row? Even games with complete information can be strategically challenging.

Chess is the classic example of a complete-information game in which nothing, in principle, is left to the imagination when fully rational players compete. Yet this seems absurd because chess is all about strategic imagination. Because complete information games may be quite complex, "full rationality" seems an implausible assumption. Mere mortals, less than fully rational by virtue of limited cognitive capacities—*boundedly rational* in the language of Simon (1957)—will struggle to establish how best to

---

*This determination is made by what is called *backward induction* in the game theory literature. Any player can, through introspection, determine the choice that will be made by the named player at each of the last nodes in the game (by determining the choice leading directly to the outcome with the highest payoff for that player among those outcomes available at that choice opportunity). Knowing this, a player can then move back a step and ask what choice a named player would make at the set of prior nodes—that is, those nodes that lead to the last nodes in the game. Repeating this reasoning, one can work all the way back to the initial node with which the game commences. Thus, any fully rational player can trace the path of the game and all of the choices made by fully rational named players at nodes along the path. (I have ignored probabilistic issues—like a named player who is indifferent among several branches at his or her node and thus decides probabilistically.)

play. With full rationality relaxed, imagination has some scope to operate. All individuals are constrained in their capacity to act in a fully rational fashion, but these bounds differ among individuals. We often say of the less constrained that they are more imaginative, that they can see further, that they possess vision. In this interpretation, imagination is reflected in the capacity to see more steps ahead than most of us. It is exercised in adopting "farsighted" strategies in the play of the game that less capable players cannot conceive.

Imagination is more than this, however, even in complete information settings with boundedly rational players. Imagination has to do not only with being able to see further down the game tree than your rivals but also with an ability to anticipate how those boundedly rational rivals will respond at each step along the way. Imagination is an exercise in psychology as well as strategy, reading the reactions of others (if not more actively inducing or coordinating them).

This still doesn't get to the heart of imagination which, I believe, requires moving to environments (like that in the figure) in which all the possibilities in a context of strategic interaction are not commonly known—information about the structure of the game is incomplete. A long-serving member of the US House of Representatives may be familiar with the twenty-nine standing rules of his legislative chamber; likewise, a veteran senator may know the forty-four rules of her chamber. But neither may have a strategic sense of all the possibilities that the rules permit, how the rules interact with one another, and where the line is drawn between what the rules permit and what they prohibit in some particular context. Indeed, each chamber appoints a parliamentarian and endows him or her with staff and resources to keep track of the precedents that determine permissible and impermissible actions. Moreover, even though the resources of the Office of the Parliamentarian are made available to all legislators in the body, some members in each body specialize in the subtleties of the chamber rules. They are known for their expertise in this respect and often make this expertise widely available to their fellow legislators.*

The exercise of imagination, in my opinion, comes in the form of devising strategies for accomplishing some purpose that other institutional colleagues could not devise on their own. In terms of a game like those just discussed, imagination arises when an agent identifies branches (moves) that emanate from a node in the game tree that other agents had not realized were available or combines a set of moves (strategies) that others had not contemplated. The incompleteness in knowledge about the game, that is, is reflected in variation among institutional agents in their knowledge about the nodes and branches consistent with the rules of the game. This is what the figure captures—that agent 2 can see things about the strategic environment of which agent 1 is unaware. When knowledge of the game is not common or complete, the game is amenable to applications of imagination by those with a subtler grasp of the possibilities.

The notion that imagination has scope to operate because some agents know more than others about the strategic setting and the opportunities it offers allows a distinction between imagination and rule breaking. Suppose a legislative game begins with an agent recognized to make a motion. A second agent is recognized who has the option to second the motion. Contingent on a motion being made and seconded, a third recognized agent may offer an amendment to the original motion, may call the previous question (forcing a vote on whether to close deliberation and vote on the motion on the floor), may move to adjourn (suspending legislative action altogether), or may assassinate the motion-maker. But where is it written in the rules of the game that the third agent may shoot the motion-maker? The plain fact

---

*For a fascinating study of the effects of making the precedents of the US House publicly known, an event occurring with their publication in 1899, see Lawrence (2013).

is that this action is *not* part of the rules. However, on some interpretations of games, the choices available to a named individual at a node are, in fact, anything that is physically possible at that point in the proceedings. Implicitly, we designate some of the branches emanating from a node as permissible according to the rules but only *some* of the branches. A clever agent may realize, as other of his colleagues do not, that some particular actions are permissible. This is imagination at work. However, the choice of other actions, available in principle but inconsistent with the rules, is to break the rules. Thus, imagination entails selecting moves that others had not realized were available; they may or may not be compatible with the rules. Rule breaking entails selecting rule-inconsistent moves.

In the essays of the next two parts, we will encounter exercises of both imagination and rule breaking. These are not mutually exclusive: both imaginative agents and rule breakers travel to parts of the game tree that others had not contemplated or even envisaged.

Part II
Institutions, Rule Breaking, and Imagination

· 3 ·

Thick Institutions
and Rule Breaking

SULLA AND CAESAR,
REED AND JOHNSON

Obeying rules and breaking rules are part of the human condition. Since time immemorial, human societies have governed themselves by rules but not with consistency and not without exception. Cicero in 66 BCE, for example, observed that "our ancestors have always followed precedent in peace, but expediency in war" (cited in Lintott 1999, 5). Ackerman (1991) notes three watershed occasions in which US history records major violations of established law: (1) the creation of the US Constitution in violation of revision procedures laid out in the Articles of Confederation; (2) the acceptance of the Reconstruction amendments without following established procedures for amending the Constitution; and (3) the reversal by the New Deal Supreme Court of established understandings of economic provisions in the Constitution,* again without observing a formal amendment procedure.

In some instances, a violation of the rules may be thought of, generously, as envelope-pushing, that is, as attempts to extend a contemporaneous practice or interpretation in a novel manner. In other instances, a violation is more brazen. In any substantive case, however, it is important to recognize that there are two elements at play: a context and an individual or group poised to take strategic action. In this essay, drawing on some prominent

---

* Particularly the sanctity of contract—see chapter 11.

settings and even more prominent individuals, I examine a range of rule-breaking instances. By emphasizing both context and individual, I mean to bring attention to the fact that obeying rules and breaking them are sometimes the norm and sometimes the exception. Individuals are provided strategic openings (or imaginatively create such openings), which they sometimes seize even if fidelity to rules is dodgy, but at other times they waver. The four men who are the subject of this chapter did not waver when opportunities presented themselves.

Sulla and Caesar were major figures in the dying decades of the Roman Republic, one of the earliest and most successful formal constitutional orders. In the late nineteenth century, Thomas Brackett Reed dominated the US House, a body suffused with rules and precedents (codified by Asher Hinds in 1899, and thereafter known simply as *Hinds' Precedents*). Lyndon Johnson led a rule-governed but norm-driven US Senate in the mid-twentieth century. All of these are "thickly institutionalized" settings, by which I mean settings in which rules of action and procedure are detailed, often of long standing, and in which most individuals most of the time expect most other individuals to observe the rules most of the time. While rule breaking might be anticipated in less thickly institutionalized settings, perhaps out of ignorance or because a rule has not buttressed expectations of widespread compliance, the stories told in this essay are of rule breaking in settings in which compliance and credible enforcement are the norm.

Sulla and Caesar

I begin with the Roman Republic, a constitutional order that lasted, in one form or another, for nearly five centuries until destroyed by civil war sparked by Caesar marching an army across the Rubicon and into Rome in 49 BCE. For five years Caesar ruled, ultimately as "dictator for life," until his assassination in 44 BCE.

The Roman Republic of this period was highly institutionalized, with legislative, executive, judicial, and ceremonial functions and powers clearly specified and widely distributed. Or so it seemed on paper. The widespread existence of veto points generated by the separation of powers meant that gridlock was always just over the horizon, that coalitions had to be assembled, often on an ad hoc basis, in order to govern, and that extralegal actions were often taken. The latter took many forms. Bribery and intimidation were two of the more common. Much money and property changed hands on a regular basis; political and military office (and their associated powers) were standard means of wealth accumulation. Judicial extortion was another form of extraordinary action: trumped-up charges and associated threats of imprisonment, exile, or death were the instruments with which to coerce those with authority to act or those with veto power to relent. And there were myriad other more direct methods of eliminating opponents altogether. If the institutions of the Roman Republic were glorious, they were also incredibly corrupt by their end. Both Sulla in the second decade of the first century BCE and Caesar some forty years later took the bull by the horns, marching armies into Rome to bring down what they considered corrupt opposition.

Sulla had throughout his life been inclined toward support of conservative politics and opposition to more populist approaches. However, he had not pursued a domestic political career or been involved in capitol politics for the most part, spending much of his adult life in various forms of military service, mainly outside Rome. Winning in the field, however, required allies in Rome. And politicians in Rome saw associations with generals in charge of armies in the field as sources of wealth and domestic political power. As a consequence, military campaigns, nominally part of the foreign policy and imperial ambition of the Republic, were inextricably bound up in domestic power struggles in the capital. Dealings, bargains, pacts, and coalitions were corrupt and corrupting. The military ambitions of Sulla—especially his desire to be the one to achieve a comprehensive victory over King Mithridates, long-standing enemy of Rome—were hamstrung by competing political interests in the capital. Time and time again, Sulla was forced to return from the field to Rome to reinforce the coalition supporting his military operations. At one point, in 87 BCE, the Roman Senate, dominated by Sulla's opponents, stripped him of his military command and handed it over to his greatest rival. Sulla, in response, marched several legions of his army to Rome, violating a long-standing and robust requirement that armies were not permitted within the city limits. He vanquished what little physical opposition existed; dealt with his opponents via jail, exile, or execution; and reestablished his military leadership.

Having restored the power of friendly politicians in Rome, Sulla set out again in his pursuit of Mithridates. During the ensuing four years, in a campaign in which Mithridates was finally vanquished, new political enemies in Rome emerged, ambitious for control of their own. Once again, the Senate relieved Sulla of command, only to find Sulla unwilling to comply. In 83 BCE, for a second time he gathered up legions to march on Rome. Despite the leadership in Rome fielding armies of its own, Sulla and his allies defeated them in battles in what had become a full-blown civil war. With all his enemies dead or escaped into exile, Sulla marched into Rome (again), took command of political institutions, and had himself named *dictator* by the Senate.

By historical practice, a Roman dictator was an individual named by the consuls (executives) with the consent of the Senate for a fixed term to deal with some omnipresent crisis—an insurrection, an invasion, a food crisis, an epidemic.* The dic-

---

*There is some speculation (see Ferejohn 2013) that the dictator institution emerged in response to the gridlock that had developed with the evolution of assemblies and officials representing the plebeians. With widely distributed veto power among plebeian and patrician institutions, there were occasions in which a more decisive response to a looming crisis was required. However, as Ferejohn

tator was "authorized to suspend rights and legal processes and to marshal military and other forces to deal with the threat of invasion or insurrection for the purposes of resolving the threat to the republic. When he finished his job [after a period of no more than six months] he was expected to step down" (Ferejohn 2013, 3). That is, once the exceptional circumstance had passed, usually after no more than six months, the dictator returned constitutional powers to the Senate and other Roman officials. In no case could the dictator move beyond his charge of resolving the crisis. He was specifically prohibited from altering constitutional arrangements.

Not so in the case of Sulla. The charge from the Senate, entirely manipulated by Sulla, was to grant the dictator not only the power to restore order in Rome after the civil war but also the authority to engage in constitutional reform. Rules and long-standing practices governing the dictator institution went out the window as Sulla first conducted a reign of terror eliminating thousands of those who had previously opposed him (including, ironically, the family of the young Julius Caesar, many of whom he imprisoned or exiled). Then, with the political field more to his liking, he remade many Roman political arrangements, not least of which were a vast expansion of the Senate (stacked with his sympathizers), restrictions on qualifications for holding political office, and a reduction of the veto power of various plebeian institutions—constitutional changes that dictators had traditionally been prohibited from making. Thus, an individual who broke the rules of military engagement—twice marching armies into the city of Rome and intimidating existing elites—went on to break the rules governing dictatorial rule. He ruled like a modern-day dictator (with the possible exception that he voluntarily stepped

---

goes on to suggest, in the latter part of the Republic's history, politics had become sufficiently divisive and dysfunctional that it was difficult for the Senate even to appoint dictators. See also Nippel (1995), Ferejohn and Pasquino (2004), and Posner (forthcoming).

down and restored normal, though now revised, politics). While some of his constitutional innovations were reversed after his death, many survived decades until the end of the Republic.*

For Julius Caesar, Sulla was a role model (up to a point—he chastised Sulla for voluntarily resigning his dictatorship). When Sulla seized power at the end of the 80s BCE, some of Caesar's relatives had been opponents necessitating young Julius's escape from Rome and into hiding. Sulla eventually absolved him, allowing Caesar to begin a military career in Asia. Thus, like Sulla, Caesar's early career was as a soldier, but he engaged more fully in Roman political life.

With military glory secured after a decade in the field, he returned to Rome to enter political life, first as a court advocate, then in various junior and senior executive positions. In 59 BCE, he allied with Pompey and Crassus, the latter providing him with immense resources with which to bribe his way to the consulship (one of two chief executives). Subsequently, his ally Pompey brought troops to Rome in order to intimidate Caesar's co-consul, Bibulus. The latter retired to his villa outside the city, freeing Caesar to govern on his own in violation of the dual-executive provisions of the Roman constitution.

Following his one-year consulship, Caesar and his Senate allies arranged for him to serve as governor of provinces in Gaul, thereby maintaining immunity from prosecution for the illegalities he committed during his consulship. During this period, he secured considerable glory and wealth through political extortion and military triumphs. In 50 BCE, with the Senate controlled by his opponents, with his financial supporter Crassus dead, and with his other former ally Pompey now consul and supporting the other side, Caesar was ordered by the Senate to stand down from his governorship and leader of his troops in Gaul and return to Rome (where he would no longer enjoy immunity from prose-

---

*He died in 78 BCE, a year after leaving politics. His epitaph read, "No friend ever served me, and no enemy ever wronged me, whom I have not repaid in full."

cution). Perceiving this as a plot by his enemies to eliminate him, he refused and was officially charged with insubordination and treason. To that he responded by marching troops toward Rome, famously crossing the Rubicon River ("the die is cast").

The civil war was on, and with Caesar victorious, the Republic was effectively ended. Over the next several years, Caesar arranged to be appointed dictator (multiple times, the last "dictator for life"), consul (multiple times, often without a co-consul), and censor (with the power to appoint new senators). These appointments entailed massive amounts of corruption—bribery of senators, massive expansion of the Senate to increase the ranks of supporters, and most significantly the concentration of executive, legislative, and judicial powers in his person in violation of the constitution's separation-of-powers arrangement. Following Caesar's assassination in 44 BCE, supporters and opponents fought another civil war, pitting assassins Brutus and Cassius against Mark Antony and Caesar's nephew Octavian. With the assassins vanquished, there was yet another conflict, this time between the victors. Octavian prevailed and, renamed Augustus, became the first emperor of the successor regime to the Republic.

Like his predecessor Sulla, Caesar's military and political careers were glorious and corrupt at the same time. In particular, his use of bribery and intimidation to gain political power, and his exercise of that political power for self-aggrandizement, made a mockery of the constitution of the Roman Republic.

What should be underscored here is that the rule breaking of Sulla and Caesar took place in a society that had been well ordered by a constitution for centuries. The constitution was not written down, but its conventions nevertheless coordinated political and social life. Elites, and citizens generally, expected the order imagined by the conventions of the constitution to be observed. And for many centuries, they mainly were.* However, in the last century

---

* The dictator institution, for example, dates to the fifth century BCE when the aristocrat farmer Cincinnatus was called upon to serve as dictator in order to vanquish

of the Republic, in spite of these expectations, there were notable violations to be sure but many petty ones as well. These violations, in turn, had feedback effects on expectations. The coordinating role of constitutional conventions was weakened. The anticonstitutional interventions of Sulla and Caesar took place in a context of diminished expectations of constitutional observance provoked by the very fact of frequent petty violations. Indeed, Sulla and Caesar each justified their own actions as serving the purpose of saving the Republic from the flood of corruption and petty violations of conventions that existed. However, this may have been no more than a convenient rationale. As Machiavelli observed in his *Discourses* (book I, chapter 34) a millennium and a half later, "if a usage is established of breaking institutions for good objectives, then under that pretext they will be broken for evil ones."* The politics of the first-century BCE Roman Republic had become the raw pursuit of advantage by legal means or otherwise. Rules were broken—in the large and in the small—because the rules were already broke. This was the context in which political entrepreneurs sought extraordinary, extraconstitutional solutions.

Reed and Johnson

Two millennia later, in another society well ordered by a constitution and a rich constellation of institutional practices, we observe more modern versions of rule breaking. Neither late-nineteenth-century US House Speaker Thomas Brackett Reed nor

---

rival tribes threatening Rome. He reluctantly took up the task, defeated the tribes, and then resigned his post to return to his farm. This established a reference point for the norm or rule that dictatorship was a *temporary* post. Likewise, the revolt against the Decemvirs—a group of ten patricians who codified and then implemented administrative law in the early Roman Republic but refused to relinquish their power—established the normative expectation that "king-like" behavior was incompatible with the republican form.

*Cited in Ferejohn and Pasquino (2004).

midtwentieth-century US Senate minority leader Lyndon Baines Johnson marched armies into Washington, but rather used their respective bully pulpits alongside sweet reason to convince their followers to follow their respective leads, despite the dubious basis on which they proceeded.

In the last two decades of the nineteenth century, the majority party in the US House, whether Democratic or Republican, often had a razor-thin margin. Under these circumstances, it was hampered in the conduct of business by two minority party tactics. First, because the Constitution and House precedents require that a quorum, consisting of a majority of the chamber, participate in any vote (with a majority of that majority prevailing), and because the majority party could not always guarantee the presence of a quorum on its own given its small advantage and inability to turn out all its members, the minority party could simply refuse to vote on an issue before the chamber. As long as the majority party could not round up all its troops and keep them cohesive, a quorum would not be present. Known as the *disappearing quorum*, this minority tactic had, for some decades, stymied the conduct of business whenever the majority party's margin was small.* In January 1890, on a bill involving a contested election, the Democratic minority's members refused to vote, simply answering "present" when their names were called rather than "yea" or "nay." The sum of votes, for and against, did not constitute a quorum. Reed ordered the clerk to mark as counting toward a quorum all those in the chamber who refused to vote, something no previous Speaker had ever done and surely something that the rules of the House at the time had not sanctioned. After three days of chaos, the Speaker prevailed, and six days after that, he introduced the "Reed Rules" permitting this new method and thus ending the disappearing quorum tactic.

A second dilatory tactic practiced by the minority party was to

---

*In 1849, more than one hundred roll-call votes were required before those casting a vote constituted a quorum on the California statehood bill.

introduce procedural motions and points of order requiring a ruling from the chair that could be appealed to the entire chamber. The latter required a roll-call vote that took nearly an hour to complete (and from which minority party members could withhold a vote). Over and over again, such delaying tactics were employed to prevent the majority from prevailing. While the majority might ultimately succeed, it was not without its cost in available plenary time; consequently, there were occasions when the majority simply withdrew a measure from consideration as the lesser of evils. Reed, again without authority from the rules, put an end to this practice as well. In order to introduce a motion or make a point of order, a member must be recognized by the chair. The chair, according to the rules, had only limited discretion in whom he recognized—mainly when more than one member was seeking recognition at the same time. Once the chair ruled on recognition, it could not be appealed. Reed took this discretion a step further by querying a member seeking recognition, "For what purpose does the gentleman rise?" If Reed determined that the purpose was obstruction, he would refuse recognition, again something contrary to contemporary practice.

The rules had not conferred on the Speaker the authority to deny recognition on substantive grounds, just as it had not conferred on him the right to his notion of what constituted a quorum. However, as Reed had articulated on many occasions, the purpose of the majority is to govern, and he expanded the powers of the chair—ending the disappearing quorum, restricting dilatory tactics—with this aim in mind. These are not the brazen rule-breaking moves of a dictator, though Reed earned the moniker "Czar" for his efforts. Reed did not march a private army into the House chamber; he did not exile or execute his opponents as Sulla and Caesar had done. Nevertheless, in a parliamentary body rich in rules and precedents, a body in which the "rule of law" was routinely observed and routinely expected to be observed, these moves by Speaker Reed were highly controversial.

Less controversial, arguably "envelope-pushing" rather than rule breaking, were the organizational decisions taken by minority leader Lyndon Baines Johnson in 1953.* Lyndon Johnson was elected to the US Senate in 1948. By 1950, he was the Democratic Whip, and because of election defeats of the incumbent leader and his successor in the 1950 and 1952 elections, Johnson was elevated to party leader in 1953. The Democrats were the minority party in this midcentury Congress.

The Senate of 1953, as other senates of this period, was dominated by an "inner club" of long-serving, mainly southern Democratic senators in coalition with long-serving Republicans. On the Democratic side, the de facto chairman of this club was Richard Russell, conservative senator from Georgia. The nominal party leader was in reality the agent of Russell and his club colleagues. And this was apparent, or so it seemed, in Johnson's elevation.

The senates of this period were also clubs in the sense that a set of informal norms—unofficial rules of the game enforced unofficially—overlaid the formal rules by which the body proceeded. Matthews (1960), calling them "folkways," identified six: apprenticeship, specialization, focus on legislative work, courtesy, reciprocity, and institutional patriotism. Newly elected senators were expected to learn about the Senate and to specialize in particular policy areas. All senators were to be "work horses not show horses," to interact with fellow senators courteously, to trade favors and otherwise reciprocate one another's support, and finally to protect the reputation and influence of the Senate (from the predations of the executive branch and the other chamber).

One of the consequences of these norms was to put considerable weight on respect for seniority. Seniority is the direct descendent of the apprenticeship norm. (Perhaps it was the other way around. In any case, they mutually reinforced each other.)

*For excellent coverage of the Johnson years in the US Senate, see Caro (2002) and Schickler (2012).

Together with specialization, it gave deference and influence to senior party members in various policy jurisdictions, the most visible indication of which was the automatic elevation of the most senior party member on a committee to leadership—chair if the party were in the majority or ranking member if the party were in the minority. Seniors were accorded other privileges as well, ranging from recognition on the floor to priority in the assignment of space in the Senate office buildings and "hideaways" in the Capitol building to privileged parking spaces.

Chief among these were the advantages enjoyed by seniors in the committee assignment process. Incumbent senators at the outset of a new Congress already enjoyed committee assignments held over from the previous Congress and, unless the party's share of seats on a committee were drastically reduced as a consequence of an election that went very badly for the party, they would continue to enjoy these—they are almost akin to a property right. There are times, however, when a senior throws his or her hat into the ring along with newly elected senators, seeking either to trade in current assignments for new ones or simply to acquire additional ones for their portfolio. In the mid-century Senate in which Lyndon Johnson had recently been elevated to party leader, the normal practice was to give preference to senior senators' requests over those of newly elected senators for initial assignments. This meant that the plum assignments were monopolized by senior senators. In particular, the so-called "big four" committees—Appropriations, Armed Services, Finance, and Foreign Relations—were senior preserves.

Lyndon Johnson, still wet behind the ears as senators go, yet ambitious beyond those brief years, determined to make the job of party leader (indeed, of *minority* party leader) something more than a mere agent of the "real" powers in the Senate, the members of the inner club. And to do this, he cast about for alternative bases of power (while being sure to keep the seniors who ran the place on board). The most underprivileged, and therefore the ripest for recruitment, were the junior members of his party (who tended to be nonsouthern and politically liberal and therefore not members of the inner club themselves). Johnson enunciated a rule—that sixty years later is still referred to as the Johnson Rule—that no senator would receive a second appointment to a big four committee until other senators requesting appointments to one of these were selected. The most important committees in the Senate would no longer, under Johnson's management, be reserved exclusively for seniors. At the time, this seemed only a minor breach in the seniority norm; indeed, it hardly affected current members of the inner club (who already held positions on the major committees). But a breach it was in what would turn out to be the opening volley in a more profound alteration of seniority practices in the Senate. The brilliance of Lyndon Johnson was in expanding his base of power while keeping his former allies on the reservation. The latter did not insist on enforcing the seniority norm as it had been previously cast. Johnson had broken an unwritten rule of the Senate and had gotten away with it.

In the highly institutionalized House of the late nineteenth century and Senate of the midtwentieth, bodies that were rule-governed because everyone mostly followed rules that they had adopted and expected others to do so as well, there was still room for institutional entrepreneurs like Reed and Johnson to violate old rules and make up new ones. They got away with this because decisive coalitions in their respective chambers wanted them, or permitted them, to do what they did. Dysfunctional behavior by minorities in Reed's House and inflexible practices in Johnson's Senate provided opportunities for legislative imagination.

The question remains as to why decisive coalitions tolerated, even supported, these departures—from written rules in Reed's case and from unwritten ones in Johnson's case. I think the answer in large part is that decisive coalitions wanted their respective leaders to succeed generally, and saw these particular departures as the price to pay for this objective. Reed's illegal actions were made legal after the fact. He not only got away with violating existing rules, but he also managed to have them become the new institutional status quo; a decisive coalition, that is, first failed to punish the departure and then decided to make the departure the way of the future. In the elections of November 1890, after the Reed Rules had been established, the Democrats won the House and revoked them. Reed's Republicans, now in the minority, began engaging in precisely the practices that the Reed Rules had meant to disable; after some time of suffering at the hands of minority obstructionist tactics, the Democrats reinstated the Reed Rules. Majorities, as Reed had observed, were meant to govern, and the Reed Rules—as seen by both Republicans and (eventually) Democrats—were the vehicle to accomplish this aim more effectively.

The tolerance of decisive coalitions for the Johnson norm violation is a bit less clear because the violation of a norm is subversive in only a weak sense. Because the violation was not immediately very costly to the inner club, and perhaps also because the party was only in the minority at the time, it was unclear to contemporaries whether Johnson's move to assuage junior, nonsouthern, liberal Democrats was an entering wedge in a full-blown assault on seniority or only a one-off move of marginal significance. Because members of the inner club thought of Johnson as almost one of them, and certainly as "their man," they wouldn't have wanted to undermine his leadership at its very beginning.

*   *   *

I have chosen to start off this part of the volume with instances of rule breaking in thickly institutionalized settings because these are the settings in which rule making and rule following are normally "the way things are done around here." Institutional rules are, in a sense, the equilibrium in place, and in the particular settings described above, they may be thought of as having been the settled mode of political practice. Things began to become unhinged in the first-century BCE Roman Republic—persistent, petty violations of constitutional norms punctuated by major disruptions during which the constitution was in suspended animation. But this happened against the backdrop of several centuries of institutional robustness. The late-nineteenth-century House was a victim of its own rules which handcuffed the majority. The norms of the midtwentieth-century Senate were unyielding at a time of social and political change in the wider society. Each of these contexts posed a challenge to the "proper order" formerly provided by existing institutions and thus presented an opportunity to enterprising political entrepreneurs. The combination of large-scale challenges to the existing order and imaginative political leadership are the occasions in which rule breaking materializes.

· 4 ·

Breaking Rules in Breaking the Filibuster

The rules governing debate in the US Senate make it one of the most distinctive legislative chambers in the world. And these, in turn, hinge on another unique Senate feature—the manner in which rules are adopted and maintained in the first place, "rules governing rules" so to speak. The US Senate is not only one of the most rule-bound political institutions in contemporary democratic practice. To further complicate matters, its rules and precedents possess an opaqueness that countenances few masters. This gives room for the gifted few to maneuver imaginatively. This and the next two essays will attempt to capture some of these accomplished performances on the Senate stage.*

Some History

First, I must prepare the ground by sketching the history of Senate rules. In the beginning, there was the constitutional mandate that "Each House may determine the Rules of its Proceedings . . ." (Article I, Section 5). The Constitution designated each chamber as a self-governing body. The early senates, despite be-

---

*The historiography and political science of the Senate and its procedures has had many important contributions. Especially illuminating are Binder and Smith (1997), Wawro and Schickler (2006), Koger (2010), and an American Political Science Association Madison Lecture and review essay by Mayhew (2003, 2010).

ing relatively small bodies, nevertheless managed to accumulate an excessively complex set of rules, mainly crafted by Thomas Jefferson during his vice presidency. These were streamlined in 1806, an exercise seen as mere "housekeeping" but with a fateful consequence. The mechanism for the body to bring itself to the stage of voting on a matter before it—for example, a motion "to call the previous question"—was inadvertently (?) omitted. Gold and Gupta (2004, 215-16), quoting Vice President Aaron Burr as recorded in the memoir of John Quincy Adams, observe, "As then-Senator John Quincy Adams reported, Burr advised [during the 1806 revision deliberations] that the motion for the previous question was of no use and should be dropped

> [Burr] mentioned one or two rules which appeared to him to need a revisal, and recommended the abolition of that respecting the *previous question*, which he said had in the four years been only taken once, and that upon an amendment. This was proof that it could not be necessary . . . [emphasis in original]

The Senate followed this advice but failed to impose any other device by which debate might be restricted. Thus, by sheer oversight in 1806, the Senate opened itself to the possibility of filibuster." This meant that the only way to proceed to a vote was by unanimous consent; otherwise, debate on the matter would continue or the Senate would suspend its deliberations on the matter and move to other business.

For more than a century, until Senate rules were changed, the unanimous-consent mechanism for closing debate and moving to a vote remained in force. In 1917, with Europe at war and the United States a neutral, President Woodrow Wilson proposed legislation to arm merchant ships to enable them to protect against attack on the high seas by any of the warring parties. A group of Republican senators, led by Robert LaFollette (R-WI), prevented the bill from coming to a vote. In an address to the nation, Wilson railed against this obstructionism in an attempt to rally public opinion: "A little group of willful men, representing no opinion but their own, have rendered the great Government of the United States helpless and contemptible."

The public backlash against the Senate was sufficient to induce both parties to collaborate in reforming the rules of debate. The new mechanism, a revision of Rule XXII, would allow debate to come to a close (known as "cloture") if supported by two-thirds of those present and voting. No longer could the Senate be held hostage by "a little group of willful men." But one-third plus one of those voting could prevent a vote from taking place. Interestingly, for half a century, even when the opposition had a sufficient quota of votes, the *filibuster* (as obstructing a path to a vote came to be known) was rarely resorted to, its use mainly restricted to southern obstruction of bills related to race. Even highly controversial legislation that often divided the parties—tariffs, executive reorganization, Roosevelt's court-packing plan—was allowed a path to a vote. Nevertheless, the filibuster was always a threat—a club behind the door so to speak—and we can't be certain that many prospective bills were never brought forward at all because of this threat.*

Although only rarely used, the very possibility of a filibuster generated substantial political frustration. From 1949 onward, at the opening of almost every Congress, a resolution to revise the rules, especially the filibuster rule, was introduced and debated only to be blocked because a supermajority was unwilling to close debate on the rules-revision proposal. In 1959, the Senate went a step further (backward?), not only retaining the existing supermajority requirement for closing debate but also adding a proviso on the continuation of rules from one Congress to the next unless revised by procedures laid out in the current rules.

---

*For some possible explanations of this pattern, see Mayhew (2003).

Specifically, Rule V.2 states: "The rules of the Senate shall continue from one Congress to the next Congress unless they are changed *as provided in these rules*" (emphasis added).

Further efforts to revise the rules over the next sixteen years consistently ran up against Rule V.2 and Rule XXII. Any measure to revise the Senate rules required compliance with *existing* Senate rules for amending the rules; therefore, it was subject to a filibuster necessitating the support of two-thirds of those present and voting to bring the measure to a final vote. Many efforts to revise the filibuster were victims of the Rule V.2 provision. Mayhew (2003) speculates that a successful revision of the filibuster rule might have occurred in the 1960s if sufficient votes to end obstruction had not been rounded up to pass the 1964 Civil Rights Act or the 1965 Voting Rights Act. But Rule XXII survived into the 1970s.

The 1975 Rules Revision

In 1975, however, there was a modicum of success. The 1975 revision resulted in a reduction in the cloture requirement to "three-fifths of those duly chosen and sworn" for ordinary motions—sixty votes in a Senate with no vacancies—and "two-thirds of those present and voting" for a revision of the rules, in each case a quorum participating. What is of relevance to the issue of rule breaking is the method by which this was accomplished.* Another dive into the weeds is required.

Senate Resolution 4 was introduced by Walter Mondale (D-MN) and James Pearson (R-KS). It sought to reduce the cloture requirement for *all* measures to three-fifths of those present and voting, a quorum present. To expedite matters, Pearson proposed a procedural motion to deal with S. Res. 4. It required that his procedural motion be voted on immediately with no debate

*The full details are found in Gold (2008).

and that its passage (by a simple majority) then required that the Senate proceed directly to vote on S. Res. 4, again without debate. In effect, Pearson's procedure would violate existing Senate rules because it would allow a *simple majority* to determine to move directly to a vote on S. Res. 4 without properly closing debate (which, according to Senate rules at the time required the support of two-thirds of those present and voting).

Majority leader Mike Mansfield (D-MT) raised a point of order against Pearson's procedure, citing Rule V.2 and the continuing nature of Senate rules. He claimed that quite apart from his own views on the filibuster, Senate rules prohibit the procedure provided by the Pearson motion. A motion, in Mansfield's view, cannot deny the application of existing rules. In particular, the motion cannot avoid the application of Rule XXII of the existing rules for shutting off debate. Vice President Nelson Rockefeller, presiding over the Senate, submitted Mansfield's point of order to the full chamber. Before a vote was taken on whether to table the point (which would reject Mansfield's objection), Rockefeller was asked whether, if Mansfield's point were rejected, he will then follow the procedure outlined in Pearson's motion. Rockefeller responded that his interpretation of events would lead him to affirm these procedures because the Senate's act in tabling the point of order in effect gives him the green light to do so.

If this seems confusing to the reader, it also did to Senator James Allen (D-AL), the master parliamentary expert of the era (see the next chapter). He pointed out to Rockefeller the inconsistency of his interpretation. How can the Senate follow the procedure provided in the Pearson motion when it hasn't even agreed to the Pearson motion yet? Defeating the Mansfield point of order, in Allen's view, would still require Pearson's motion, like any other, to be taken up under existing rules, in particular under the direction of Rule XXII, because the Senate is a continuing body according to Rule V.2 (citing the reaffirmation of this position in the last rules revision in 1959). Gold (2008, 61) puts it thus: "In other words, how can the Senate be bound by the terms of a motion it [merely] refused to [accept a point of order against] but has not yet adopted?" In Allen's view, even if Mansfield's objection failed, the Senate still had to vote directly on the Pearson proposal before it could proceed to consider S. Res. 4. Rockefeller stood his ground, stating that by defeating the Mansfield point of order, the Senate is expressing its willingness to proceed in this manner. Gold (2008, 61) continues, "Although Pearson's motion *runs contrary to the Senate rules*, Rockefeller will abide by it because, when it tabled Mansfield's point of order, the Senate expressed its will that he do so" (emphasis added). The Senate, by simple majority, did table Mansfield's point of order. After some political negotiations, a revised version of S. Res. 4 passed. The revision allowed for debate on "normal" bills to be brought to a close with the support of "three-fifths of those duly elected and sworn," while cloture on bills proposing changes in the rules themselves to require the support of "two-thirds of those present and voting."

For the rest of this story, the reader should consult Gold (2008, 60-68). For our purposes, the interesting things to note are, first, that the rules specify the Senate is a continuing body—the rules of the Senate in one Congress carry over to the next Congress—and, second, that its rules for amending the rules must follow the procedures laid out in those existing rules. Nevertheless, a majority, by sustaining the "illegal" (i.e., rule-breaking) interpretation of the Pearson motion by presiding officer Rockefeller, may choose to violate its own rules. The filibuster was modified, but only because the rules were broken.

Epilogue

In 2013, after several Congresses in which Republican majorities in the House and minorities in the Senate frustrated the ambitions of Democratic president Barack Obama, majority patience in the Senate wore thin. In a set of parliamentary maneuvers, the Democrats, by a simple majority vote, revised the Senate rules to allow the closing of debate on presidential nominations (except to the Supreme Court) by a simple majority vote. Minority leader Mitch McConnell (R-KY), expressing his own frustration at the dubious parliamentary moves by the majority, despite a very clear Rule XXII (as revised in 1975) governing cloture, observed, "If the majority can't be expected to follow the rules, then there aren't any rules" (quoted in *New York Times*, December 11, 2013, p. A18). Rule breaking provides a short-term fix to a procedural dilemma but may have the longer-term consequences of more rule breaking, a diminished legitimacy accorded previous ways of conducting business, and a great deal of self-imposed uncertainty over exactly what game is being played.

· 5 ·

Political Imagination after Filibuster Reform

THE POSTCLOTURE FILIBUSTER AND ITS DEMISE

A new set of rules means a new game. The 1975 revision of Senate Rule XXII just recounted changed the legislative playing field. Legislation that would have failed the two-thirds cloture threshold of the old rule might now pass the three-fifths requirement of the new one. Sponsors deterred by the old standard from even introducing a bill might be encouraged by the more relaxed standard to push ahead. The obstructionist opportunities of intense minorities had been diminished.

However, new rules invite imaginative new strategies. The 1975 reform in the filibuster rule provided incentives for the invention of clever parliamentary tactics. The master was James Allen (D-AL) who invented the *postcloture filibuster*. According to the filibuster rule newly in place, once cloture is secured, each senator is limited to one hour of speaking time, thus allowing for up to one hundred hours of further discussion before a vote must be taken. But the rule did not obviate the need to dispose of amendments to the measure that had already been introduced or limit the number of those amendments (so long as an amendment was germane and had been introduced before the cloture vote). Additionally, it did not limit the reading of amendments, quorum calls, or roll-call votes. In short, there was still no practical limit on how much time could be devoted to a measure, *even after cloture had been voted*. This set of opportunities was actively utilized by Allen, bringing the Senate to a standstill on many occasions. In advance of a cloture motion, Allen or his collaborators would introduce a large number of amendments, imposing unbearable time costs on the proponents of a bill as well as on those whose own future priorities would be compromised by the reduction of plenary time. The postcloture tactic reached its zenith (nadir?) in 1977 when Howard Metzenbaum (D-OH) and James Abourezk (D-SD) followed the strategy fashioned by Allen. In advance of a cloture vote on a natural gas deregulation bill that they and other liberal senators opposed, they submitted hundreds of amendments. The Senate was compelled to take up these amendments after cloture had been voted, a filibuster-by-amendment maneuver lasting thirteen days. And still no senator had used his or her one hour of permitted speaking time.

Robert Byrd (D-WV), in his first year as majority leader, aimed to break this device by closing the loopholes in Rule XXII that permitted it. If he had tried to do this by introducing a rules revision, it would have been necessary, first, to secure cloture on any measure he proposed (cloture on a rules change, recall, required two-thirds support) and, second, to overcome a postcloture filibuster on his measure to end postcloture filibusters! This posed a tactical dilemma.

Byrd chose a course of action in the debate on the natural gas deregulation bill that, by reasonable interpretation, violated Senate rules. According to existing rules, a postcloture motion can be ruled out of order by the presiding officer only in response to a point of order from the floor; he does not have independent authority to do so. And any ruling by the presiding officer on a point of order can be appealed and debated, with the latter brought to a close only by a cloture vote. All of these moves and countermoves, of course, consume immense amounts of time. This is what made the postcloture filibuster tactic designed by Allen so effective. Byrd's imaginative maneuver was to secure a ruling from the presiding officer, Vice President Walter Mondale, that, postcloture, any amendment introduced before cloture had been voted, but deemed *nongermane* or otherwise inappropriate according to Senate rules, could be ruled out of order without the necessity of a point of order. (Why this ruling was not challenged, I do not know.) Having secured this general ruling on amendments, Byrd began calling up the many remaining amendments that were being used by Metzenbaum and Abourezk to obstruct consideration of the unfinished business before the Senate. Mondale would rule one out of order as defective, and before an appeal of his ruling could be made, Byrd, using his priority right of recognition as majority leader, would call up another amendment. This way, the majority leader, in cahoots with the vice president, disposed of the remaining amendments being used for obstructionist purposes in about an hour.

The parliamentary dance choreographed by the vice president and the majority leader was believed by many not to be sanctioned by the rules. Underscoring the probably underhanded maneuver by the majority leader is the fact that at the beginning of the next Congress, in January 1979, Byrd felt it necessary to amend Rule XXII formally. The new rule placed a one-hundred-hour cap on postcloture activity, thereby allowing for only limited postcloture obstruction. Note that Byrd did *not* do this in 1977, breaking the rules instead.

Allen and Byrd, like Lyndon Johnson before them, were masters of Senate procedure. Both were held in high regard by colleagues—liberals and conservatives, Democrats and Republicans—for their intimate knowledge of rules and precedents, and their strategic insight and practical advice on how to maneuver within this vast body of political regulations. Allen's approach to making postcloture mischief provided a tactical methodology for his generalized southern aversion to limitations on the filibuster. In spite of the reduced cloture requirement of the 1975 reform, he had imaginatively found a way, *within the rules*, to minimize, if not neutralize, the opportunities the reform appeared to award legislative activists. Lacking a rule-based countermeasure, and only just having been elevated to the majority leader post and not wanting an early defeat on his watch, Byrd concocted a *rule-disregarding* offset with which to thwart Allen's designs. In both cases, the rules provided a context in which to work legislative magic. Allen took the rules as given and imagined a way to use them to his advantage. He saw a previously unforeseen branch of the game tree that he used to create a new path to obstruction. Byrd cheated and then changed the rules after the fact.

· 6 ·

A Third Take on the Filibuster

BREAKING RULES BY REINTERPRETING RULES

In his 1991 book, *Information and Legislative Organization*, Keith Krehbiel gave currency to the idea of "remote majoritarianism." By this he meant that the legislative chambers of the US Congress are inherently majoritarian. At the end of the day, and in a deep sense, simple parliamentary majorities get their way. Even when the rules privilege supermajorities, the rules themselves are the product of simple majoritarian deliberation. And even when deliberation over the rules require supermajority assent to any changes, simple majorities may seek alternatives to explicit rule changes in order to accomplish their objectives.

In light of the last two chapters, the reader understandably might quibble with the idea of remote majoritarianism. The US Senate is certainly a majority-rule institution because a simple majority of senators may pass a bill (with the proviso that at least a majority of the chamber—a quorum—is present). But it may be recalled that the Senate's Rule XXII, while consistent with simple-majority determination of a vote on a bill's final passage, nevertheless requires supermajority assent to allow a bill to proceed to that vote on final passage. Forty-one determined senators in a full-quota Senate may prevent a vote on final passage (only thirty-four on a motion to alter Senate rules) by refusing to close debate. So, if a minority may obstruct a simple majority from working its will, how can Krehbiel's argument for remote majoritarianism be sustained? The answer: Where there's a will, there's a way. I will consider a role for *interpreting* the rules in which the presiding officer and chamber majorities figure prominently as interpretive agents.

Interpretation by the Presiding Officer

Senate rules are not always straightforward or transparent. In a word, they are subject to *interpretation*. And this is one of the duties performed by a presiding officer (often in consultation with the parliamentarian, an employee of the Senate appointed by the majority party). If the stars are properly aligned—that is, if the majority party in the Senate also controls the presidency so that one of its copartisans, the vice president (or another majority party senator in his stead), is the presiding officer—then there is the possibility of a majority-party-favored interpretation of a rule. That is, in a particular circumstance, the majority party may seek to work its will through a ruling from the chair—say, a ruling that a motion to table a piece of majority-party legislation (and thus kill it) is not in order.

There are still some hurdles to clear because an interpretive ruling from the presiding officer need not be the final word. If, say, one of the minority senators is unhappy with the ruling of the chair, he or she may appeal it to the full chamber, with a majority determining whether to sustain or reverse the ruling. You would think that as long as the majority party was prepared for this maneuver, the effort to derail things by reversing the ruling of the chair should easily be defeated. The majority, that is, would simply vote to sustain the ruling of the chair. The move by the minority senator, however, may be more strategic than meets the eye because the minority senator's appeal may be filibustered and a majority may not have the sixty (or sixty-seven) votes necessary to close debate on the appeal. The minority senator's real motive in appealing the ruling of the chair is to force costly delay.

Koger (2003, 4–5), a political science expert on the filibuster, writes that a simple majority has tricks up its collective sleeve to repel such strategic ploys:

> The important quality of appeals on parliamentary rulings is that a determined majority can always get a decisive vote on a ruling. First, any senator can move to table (kill) the appeal; since this motion is nondebatable the vote occurs immediately. Second, the presiding officer may listen to some discussion on the appeal and then insist that a vote take place. Third, a nonassertive presiding officer may allow unlimited debate on an appeal. In that case, any senator . . . can make a secondary point of order that debate on the appeal has gone on long enough. Since Senate rule XX requires an immediate vote when a second-tier appeal arises, this strategy allows a majority to obtain a vote on an appeal when the presiding officer is unwilling to end debate himself. Thus a majority of the Senate should always be able to reinterpret Senate rules even if senators try to filibuster the appeal.*

Koger here suggests that a sympathetic presiding officer may, through his or her interpretation of Senate rules and precedents, make rulings that facilitate the majority's agenda and overcome the obstruction of mischievous minorities. These rulings, if sustained by the chamber, become new precedents that will govern future similar deliberations (unless a future presiding officer rules otherwise). Indeed, in an effort to influence the ruling of the presiding officer in a specific instance, both sides on an issue will comb the volumes of Senate precedents for rulings of previous presiding officers that favor their interpretation.[†] The need

---

*Quotations are from Koger (2003). This paper was incorporated into a larger work, Koger (2008). Citations are to the 2003 version.

[†]Their comprehensive familiarity with rules and precedents is an important part of what gave Senators Johnson, Byrd, and Allen—all featured in previous chapters—

for interpretation gives force to the claim that rules themselves lack the clarity and certainty to convey obvious meaning to an often-complex parliamentary situation. The intervention of human agency is required.

Interpretive interventions by a presiding officer are sometimes necessary if the body of explicit rules is to avoid becoming too cumbersome. Interpretation allows general principles to be applied meaningfully to specific situations. There's hardly any argument with this view. But surely there is a line—fuzzy though it may be—separating interpretation from violation. If a rule says, "If situation A arises, then x is required," and the presiding officer acknowledges that situation A has arisen but rules "do $-x$," then it is reasonable to conclude that the line has been crossed. Interpretation may be required to determine whether situation A has indeed arisen, and it may also be required to specify exactly what "do x" means in the specific case at hand. But "do $-x$" surely does not fall within the latter category. Rather, it is interpreting the rules by breaking the rules.

A related situation is one in which the presiding officer, while not explicitly breaking a specific rule, nevertheless acts in a way not sanctioned by the rules. In effect, the presiding officer "reinterprets" his or her authority. In an earlier chapter, we saw Speaker Reed, in 1890, assume the authority to count quorums in the US House—specifically, instructing the clerk to count members present in the chamber as contributing to a quorum whether they respond to their name in a quorum call or roll-call vote or not. This reinterpreted authority only became part of the House rules after the fact, when the Reed Rules were formally adopted by the chamber. Likewise, in the previous chapter, we saw Vice President Mondale, while presiding over the Senate in 1977, declare as "defective" and thus out of order amendments

their strategic influence on the workings of the Senate. It is said that they were regular presences on the Senate floor, available to any and all for consultation on how to get something done according to the labyrinthine procedures of this body.

introduced before cloture had been secured but still on the agenda and thus normally treated as part of the chamber's unfinished business even after cloture had been voted. This, too, was authority not previously granted or normally exercised by a presiding officer of the Senate. And as in the case of Reed and the House, this authority was only formally sanctioned two years later and incorporated into Senate rules.*

Interpretation by a Simple Majority

Egregious rule breaking by a presiding officer in the Senate is rare, partly because senators abhor ceding authority to any presiding officer, especially to one assigned by the Constitution and thus not chosen by them, and partly because decisive coalitions benefit most of the time from existing rules—most of the time, but not always. Senate majorities, on the other hand, break their own rules through reinterpretation with some regularity. Koger (2003) provides a number of examples.

Here's one illustration. Senate Rule XVI states in part that "no amendment offered by any . . . Senator which proposes general legislation shall be received to any general appropriation bill, nor shall any amendment not germane or relevant to the subject matter contained in the bill be received." Senators like their appropriations measures clean—no substantive baggage in the form of new legislative proposals and no spending proposals unrelated to the subject matter of the appropriations bill. They like their spending measures clean, except when it is inconvenient.

In 1995, Senator Kay Hutchinson (R-TX) introduced an amendment to an appropriations measure that, for a set period of time, would have suspended the authority of the government to de-

---

*According to Koger (2003, table 2), the 1979 rule allowed that "after cloture is approved, the chair can rule amendments non-germane or dilatory without appeal." Mondale had exercised this authority two years before it had been allowed by the rules.

clare any new species as endangered. Senator Harry Reid (D-NV) raised a point of order asserting the amendment violated Rule XVI. The Senate rejected Reid's point by a 52–47 vote. "The effect of this precedent was to nullify Rule XVI, which prohibits policy riders ('general legislation') on appropriations bills." Koger (2003, 13) goes on to report that this precedent permitted substantive amendments to appropriations measures—an evisceration of a Senate rule via "interpretation"—that lasted four years before Republicans were able to reverse the precedent with a resolution restoring Rule XVI enforcement. A majority, through its rejection of Reid's point of order, violated one of its rules in place at the time (Rule XVI) and, in effect, *changed* its rules in an unapproved manner in violation of Rule XXII (which requires two-thirds support to alter a standing rule).

Here is another of Koger's examples involving rules governing conference committees (one I pursue more systematically in chapter 9). In order to resolve differences between versions of a bill passed by each chamber—necessitated by the Constitutional requirement that a bill pass each chamber in identical form before being presented to the president for his signature—the House and Senate often create a conference committee. This is a joint committee with separate House and Senate delegations. They deliberate on the two versions with an eye to forging a compromise conference report, which is then returned to each chamber for an up-or-down vote. Each chamber has particular rules governing how this process works. In the Senate (the House has a similar rule), Rule XXVIII states that "conferees shall not insert in their report matter not committed to them by either House, nor shall they strike from the bill matter agreed to by both Houses." In short, conferees have to work with what is presented to them, neither adding new stuff nor subtracting matters to which the two chambers have commonly agreed. But a rule can be broken if a majority permits it.

In a 1996 reauthorization of the Federal Aviation Administration, conferees added a provision that appeared in neither chamber's bill—a provision to make it difficult for employees of Federal Express to organize. The Senate allowed the provision to remain, thus gutting its own Rule XXVIII. The precedent was not reversed until the end of the 106th Congress in late 2000. The particular detail from which the precedent emerged was small potatoes compared to opening the gates to the misuse of the conference procedure over the next four years. Party leaders began the practice of attaching entirely new legislation to conference reports, legislation that had passed neither chamber. Given the protection afforded conference reports—they may either be accepted or rejected, but not amended—it would have been very painful to majorities in either chamber to defeat an entire conference report just to get rid of the offending pieces. The permitted violations of Rule XXVIII also allowed senators, through their allies on the conference committee, to insert pork-barrel projects that had not been approved through the normal legislative process.

In short, selective nonapplication of formal rules, sometimes initiated by a presiding officer and in any case sanctioned by legislative majorities, constitutes breaking rules. The rule remains on the books, but being on the books now has at best an ambiguous meaning.* It means that it will have a constraining effect on

---

*Underlining this ambiguity is another Senate practice, something of a halfway house between observing and breaking rules—a standing order. Two knowledgeable constitutional theorists put it this way: "the Senate could adopt a Standing Order altering the Senate's procedures. . . . Standing Orders are not incorporated into the text of the Standing Rules, but nonetheless bind the Senate. For example, in December 2000, the Senate adopted a standing order limiting members' ability to filibuster conference reports. The order provided that members could no longer demand the reading of conference reports that were available in writing." See Gold and Gupta, (2004, 209). The first author is a former parliamentarian of the Senate. A standing order thus "carves out" an area where rules—in this case Rule XXII—do not apply; but it does not revise the rules according to revision procedures laid out in the rules. A generous interpretation of a standing order is that it functions a bit like "suspension of the rules" in the House, but it is accomplished by only a

proceedings only if and when a majority wishes it so. It recalls
minority leader Mitch McConnell's frustration on another matter (quoted in an earlier chapter) but applies here as well: "If the
majority can't be expected to follow the rules, then there aren't
any rules."

---

simple majority, it typically is very specific about the procedure to be followed, and
it "stands" unless an explicit time limit is agreed to or it is revised by a subsequent
action by the Senate. A less generous, but possibly more accurate, interpretation
of a standing order is that it, in effect, breaks the rules by violating the prescribed
method for changing rules. A unanimous consent agreement is another way to
break the rules temporarily. It usually applies only to the situation at hand and, of
course, requires unanimity to impose.

Obstruction and Urgency in the Nineteenth-Century House of Commons

We have seen how Speaker Thomas Reed exercised considerable imagination in violating the rules of the US House of Representatives in 1890 (see chapter 4). Contrary to the powers then vested in the Office of the Speaker, Reed dealt decisively with a governance issue—minority obstruction via disappearing quorums and dilatory motions—by *inventing* the Speaker's right to regulate how quorums would be counted and to determine who would be recognized to speak or offer motions on the floor. The Speaker, in effect, asserted his right to manage the legislative process on behalf of the majority party.* These powers soon were made part of the Standing Rules of the House, rules that came to be known as *Reed's Rules*. But these powers were not part of the rules at the time Reed asserted them.†

---

*As he wittily observed in 1880, a decade before his decisive action, "The best system is to have one party govern and the other party watch; and on general principles I think it would be better for us to govern and for the Democrats to watch" (cited in Strahan 2007, 79).

†To be precise, there had been some evolution of precedents giving the Speaker authority on recognition and its protection—the Speaker's recognition or denial thereof, for example, could not be appealed. However, Reed's right to count quorums in the manner he did had not been formally established until the Reed Rules were adopted some weeks after he first employed the practice. The same may be said for Reed's practice of querying a member on the purpose for which he sought recognition in order to determine whether his purpose was dilatory. Denial of rec-

A decade earlier, another speaker, an ocean away, confronted a similar problem. Minority obstruction in the House of Commons of Great Britain had brought this august legislative assembly to its knees in 1881. Speaker of the House of Commons, Sir Henry Brand, took an unusual step in violation of regular order in the House. He closed debate on a bill that had been blocked from a vote before normal criteria for cloture had been met.* The procedural "villains" in this case were a collection of Irish members of Parliament (MPs), led by Charles Stewart Parnell; at their strongest, they amounted to no more than one-eighth of the chamber, often even less. But they had prevented any action by the chamber—not just action on Ireland-related matters but *any* action—for a considerable time. They did so by exploiting every opportunity to delay the proceedings—motions to adjourn were especially common and frequent, but other dilatory actions also existed in their arsenal, including simply making long-winded speeches on the floor.

It should be noted that the Speaker of the House of Commons, unlike his counterpart in the US House of Representatives, is not a partisan officer. He is not elected by, nor the leader of, the government of the day. Rather, as both a normative aspiration and a positive description, he is a *parliamentary* officer who presides over, rather than leads, the House. And he does so in a neutral, nonpartisan fashion. He has a stake neither in the government's program nor in anything that a parliamentary majority might wish to accomplish. His central, indeed exclusive, job is to main-

---

ognition on substantive grounds was not then within the scope of the Speaker's authority. Reed broke the rules as they existed at the time.

*Strahan (2007, 211n23) observes that Reed may have "taken inspiration from actions taken a few years earlier by the speaker of the British House of Commons to rein in minority obstructionism in that body." Of the British Speaker's decision to refuse dilatory motions or other uses of the rules to obstruct business in the House of Commons, Reed commented, "He did it without the action of the House, with no precedent in his favor, and nothing to sustain him but the common-sense of the English people."

tain proper order and, through this, the dignity of the House. Peppered throughout a typical debate in the Commons is the occasional intervention by the Speaker reminding a speech maker that a particular subject was not on point, or that his discussion had made reference to past debates, neither of which were permitted by the rules. Rarely did the Speaker intervene in other circumstances, and certainly not in any substantive manner.

In the 1870s, maintaining order and "the dignity of the House" was no mean feat. The context was one in which a parliamentary caucus, consisting of MPs elected under the banner of an Irish nationalist party founded early in the decade, had grown discouraged by its inability to capture the attention of the Commons for its cherished cause—Irish home rule. Discouraged by the disinterest of the governing majority and frustrated by the conservative tactics of its own leader, Isaac Butt, the caucus turned leadership over to a young MP who was first elected in a by-election in 1875. Charles Parnell studied past instances of obstruction, finding them ineffectual mainly because they were used so tentatively and sporadically. "It was Parnell's innovation to turn transient protest into permanent war. . . . Parnell saw himself as the 'enemy' of the House. In keeping with this view of his role, he used obstructive tactics, not simply to combat individual pieces of legislation, but to bring the entire functioning of the Parliament to a halt. In short, Parnell was the founder of 'systematic obstruction' in Parliament . . ." (Chafetz 2011, 1018–19). Or, as Dion (1997, 192) put it, "What then was so novel about Parnell's behavior? What made him stand out? For the British, it was his willingness to obstruct *all* legislation, not just those dealing with the affairs of Ireland, that made him a legislative revolutionary." Or, finally, as Josef Redlich (1908, I:137), author of the classic three-volume history of parliamentary procedure, wrote, "Parnell was . . . the inventor of a new kind of political tactics, a new expedient for gaining power in political warfare. . . . He was the founder of systematic obstruction. . . . [H]e became by his parliamentary tactics the involuntary but irresistible cause of a total reform in the conduct of business in the House."

Parnell played by the rules, using a variety of dilatory motions, legislative speeches, and other tactics that were permissible under the rules, to impede progress on legislation.* That was what so frustrated majority MPs—it was *their* rules after all.† And the majority seemed hesitant to alter them. There had been a long-standing tradition in the House of Commons of preserving the rights of minorities, especially their right to speak to the House, which Parnell exploited. But after a year or so of systematic obstruction by Parnell and his minions, some were thinking enough is enough.

In baby steps, the majority sought to bring Parnell's efforts to a halt. In 1877, for example, Speaker Brand warned Parnell that obstruction for obstruction's sake was intolerable to the chair and that he could, with provocation, hold Parnell in contempt and suspend his participation for a fixed amount of time. However, the majority lacked the will to support these penalties. Nor did they have the will even to silence a member for the duration of a specific debate if he were determined to be a serial offender of obstruction. A motion to limit dilatory motions did pass; however, the majority was loath to impose any restrictions on speech, thus preserving that channel of obstruction.

In 1880, after enduring several years of minority procedural interference, the majority adopted a new rule (a *standing order* as it is called in the Commons) that made it possible to suspend a member for a day if he were thought to be willfully obstructing chamber business, and for the suspension to escalate with mul-

---

*Parnell played the innocent, maintaining that he was not an obstructionist, and complained of a double standard in which whenever an Irish MP took an interest in English law, cries of obstruction were heard. See Dion (1997, 193) and Redlich (1908, I:144).

†As Dion (1997, 13) notes, "Minorities were after all only able to obstruct because the rules allowed them to do so."

tiple abuses. Majority governments—both the Tories until 1880 and the Liberals after that—were running out of patience with Parnell.

Impatience crested when new Liberal prime minister William Gladstone introduced the Irish Coercion Bill in 1881. This had been preceded in April 1880 by an Irish-sponsored bill that had made progress through the House to suspend foreclosures on and evictions from Irish farms. The newly installed Gladstone government, wishing to seize the initiative, introduced a Land Bill superseding the Irish-sponsored bill. This attempt, supported by the Irish MPs, was nipped in the bud in a resounding rejection by the House of Lords. Violence increased in Ireland as farmers armed themselves to prevent their farms from being seized. The hope of Parnell and his fellow Irish MPs that Gladstone would re-introduce a Land Bill went unrealized, and as violence escalated, Gladstone's government introduced its Irish Coercion Bill aimed at protecting person and property from the violence. In response, Parnell and his copartisans pushed obstruction into overdrive, causing the House to devote more than forty hours of debate to this measure—including at one point a single sitting of twenty-four straight hours—with no end in sight.

At this point, Speaker Brand had seen enough and initiated what Redlich (1908, I:153) referred to as his "celebrated coup d'état." In violation of the rules of proper order and ordinary procedure, he refused to allow any further debate, would not recognize anyone to make an additional speech, and called for a vote. In his speech to his colleagues (cited in Chafetz 2011, 1021), he observed that "the usual rules have proved powerless to ensure orderly and effective Debate. . . . A new and exceptional course is imperatively demanded; and I am satisfied that I shall best carry out the will of the House, *and may rely upon its support* [italics added], if I decline to call upon any more Members to speak, and at once proceed to put the Question from the Chair." Brand acted "on his own initiative . . . an action without precedent in the history of the Commons. . . . [He] considered it his duty as Speaker to resolve the situation and right a great indignity to the House" (Dion 1997, 208). Brand had cleared this move with Gladstone (hence the italicized phrase above), eliciting from him a commitment of support and a promise to revise the standing orders to allow for an orderly conclusion to debate in the future.

On a roll after the Speaker's intervention, Gladstone's majority approved a temporary procedure for closure (a so-called *sessional rule* that expires at the end of a parliamentary session). It involved giving the Speaker great discretion in overseeing legislative debate. In particular, it enabled a government minister to "move that a particular bill, motion, or question was urgent (hence the name 'urgency motions'). Urgency motions were not subject to debate, amendment, or a motion for adjournment, thus removing much of the potential for obstruction. If sustained in the motion by the Commons, debate [on the urgent bill] would proceed under rules to be determined by the Speaker" (Dion 1997, 209). A year later, Parliament approved a new standing order (a permanent rule that does not expire at the end of a parliamentary session) that allowed a simple majority to close debate.

Like Reed a decade later, Speaker Brand, by breaking the rules, saved an institution that was failing in its purposes. But also like Reed, Brand had the support of a majority of the chamber. The lesson here is that there are times when a decisive chamber coalition is unwilling to enforce its own rules or punish violations of them, even hallowed rules (like the protection of minority speech rights). Stable institutions must simultaneously preserve order in its procedures and protect minority participation. Sometimes these objectives clash.

· 8 ·
Violating Legislative Rules
RESOLVING BICAMERAL DIFFERENCES

As I have noted several times in previous chapters, each chamber is a self-governing, rule-creating body. In order to be a *rule-obeying* body, however, it must actually *follow* its own rules and be willing to *enforce* those rules when confronted by violations. These are things it is not always prepared to do. As we have already seen, the House permitted Speaker Thomas Reed to violate chamber rules by "innovating" the counting of quorums in the late nineteenth century; and the Senate has played fast and loose with its own rules on several occasions in the twentieth century in modifying the ways it governs debate. It is one thing for a legislative body to suspend its rules temporarily—and both the House and the Senate possess the procedural means for doing this. It is another thing for a legislative body to amend its rules—and the rules of both chambers provide procedures for this as well. However, it is an altogether different thing for a legislative body to break its rules.

In the present chapter, I take up a problem that confronts bicameral legislative bodies—namely, the challenge of bringing their respective versions of a bill into common agreement when creating a law. In the United States, the Presentment Clause of the Constitution (Article I, Section 7) requires the House and Senate to agree on a bill before it is presented to the president for his consent or veto. At the end of the day, this means the House and Senate must pass a bill in identical form—from its title down to every last comma and period. Inasmuch as the House and Senate are filled with independent-minded politicians who march to their own drummers—with different constituencies, different term lengths and electoral cycles, different political ambitions, different party attachments, and indeed, sometimes the chambers themselves controlled by different partisan majorities—this is never an easy task.

Over the decades and centuries, the two chambers have crafted alternative procedures for combining their respective efforts into a common product. There are essentially three such procedures. Each of these procedures is employed during the course of a legislative session, sometimes in combination during the consideration of a piece of legislation.

The first and simplest is for each chamber to pass a bill in identical form. The House, for example, passes a bill declaring the second Sunday in May as Mother's Day and transmits it to the Senate. The Senate, in turn, agrees to the bill. With each chamber having passed a bill in identical form, it is then forwarded to the president for his or her signature, and we are done. In the last twenty-five years, between two-thirds and four-fifths of all bills that have become public law fit this pattern. Most public laws, that is, are sufficiently simple so that arrival at chamber congruence is straightforward. And the trend is upward; increasingly, there are no differences between the chambers to resolve (when they can be gotten to act at all, not always so easy in a world in which blocking action and gridlock in each chamber is the scourge of recent years).

The second procedure, known as messaging between the chambers, or *ping-ponging*, involves passing different versions of a bill back and forth between the House and Senate until convergence is reached. To give some flavor, consider this fictitious example. The House passes a bill declaring the third Sunday in May as Mother's Day and transmits it to the Senate. The Senate agrees to the House bill with an amendment replacing "third Sunday" with "second Sunday" and returns it to the House. The House *recedes* from its version and *agrees* (both technical terms) to the Senate version with an amendment of its own, adding "and the second Monday in May as Mother's Helper's Day," and sends it back to the Senate. The Senate recedes from its version and agrees to the House version and, with both chambers now concurring in a common version, transmits it to the president for his or her signature. Although as noted above, occasions on which to resolve differences between the chambers constitute only a fraction of all legislative actions, when there are differences to resolve, ping-ponging is of growing popularity. At the end of the twentieth century, it was twice as likely as the conference procedure (described next) as the method of resolving differences. In the twenty-first century it is four times as likely.

Finally, there is the *conference procedure*. This may occur after each chamber has passed different versions of a bill and attempts to resolve these differences have failed. Or both chambers may agree to proceed to conference immediately. In effect if not in fact, at some point one of the chambers refuses to recede from its own version and instead *insists* on it—the technical term for refusing further back-and-forth bargaining. If the other chamber insists on its own version as well, then a *state of disagreement* is said to exist. At this point, one house may request a conference with the other, the aim of which is to resolve differences in their respective bills. A conference replaces the arm's-length exchange of ping-ponging with intensive face-to-face bargaining. Throughout much of the nineteenth and twentieth centuries, especially for highly complex pieces of legislation like tariff and spending bills, the two chambers wouldn't even mess around with messaging but move straight to a conference.

Once a conference has been requested by a chamber and accepted by the other, each chamber's conferees (also known as managers) are appointed. The methods of appointment have varied over time in the two chambers. Most recently, the House rules delegate appointment power to the Speaker (admonishing him or her to appoint at least some members who represent the views of the chamber as expressed in the bill it passed). The Senate, by unanimous consent, typically gives this authority to its presiding officer; however, it can withhold this authority and in its place, pass a motion naming the Senate delegation, a motion requiring only a simple majority for approval but also one that can be filibustered (if some members are looking to delay the proceedings). In each case, the robust norm is to include as conferees those most closely associated with managing the bill through their respective chambers in the first place—namely, members of the committee(s) with jurisdiction over the subjects with which the bill deals. On appropriations bills, for example, it is typical for the entire jurisdictionally relevant House and Senate subcommittees from their respective full Appropriations Committees to serve as their chamber conferees. As a result, the respective chamber delegations are often of different sizes, but this is of no ultimate consequence because approval of a final conference decision requires the support of a majority of *each* delegation (rather than a majority of the entire conference).

What is this final conference decision? The conference is a place to bargain. The final product of this bargaining is a *conference report*—a settlement of the two chamber versions of a bill. The conferees have two versions of a law before them, the one passed by the House—call it H—and the one passed by the Senate—call it S. They are charged by their respective chambers to craft a "compromise" version—call it C. This conference compromise is returned to each chamber for an up-or-down vote. Each chamber, that is, must "take it or leave it," with no amendments allowed. If both chambers approve, then the condition of the Presentment Clause will have been met, and the compromise version can be sent to the president.

Each chamber's rules, the *Standing Rules of the United States*

House and the *Standing Rules of the United States Senate*, place limits on how the conference product may be taken up in the respective chambers and what in fact the conference committee is permitted to accomplish (Rule 28 and Rule 27, respectively). There is much detail and red tape for two primary reasons. First, there are changing circumstances, the most significant being whether a conference report is taken up by the parent chambers during the dying days of a session or earlier. If a report is submitted at the end of a session, when adjournment is imminent, then the rules are a bit more permissive in allowing the chambers to reach a timely conclusion without dotting all the *i*'s or crossing all the *t*'s that would otherwise be required of the process if occurring earlier in the session.

A second reason for red tape is a regulatory purpose. Each chamber stands not only in an adversarial relationship to the other chamber but also in a somewhat tenuous and indefinite relationship to its own conferees. The chambers have worked their wills, so to speak, in producing H and S, respectively. The conferees now sitting across the table from one another are *agents* of their respective chambers, but they may not be—indeed often are not—*representative* of their respective chambers. The agents have preferences of their own, which if left unconstrained, they would seek to incorporate into the compromise, C. The two chamber rules referred to above serve precisely to constrain conferees, in effect to make sure that even if they are not precisely representative of their respective chambers, they nevertheless do not drift too far away from what the chambers would want if the chambers "themselves" could be sitting across the table from one another.

The main restriction on conference reports contained in chamber rules is known as the *scope-of-the-differences* requirement, consisting of three parts. First, the conference report must leave in place any features of H and S that are in agreement. If, for example, each bill expressly prohibits any appropriated funds to be used for some particular purpose—abortion counseling, conversion of corn into ethanol, training foreign intelligence personnel—then the prohibition must be included in C. The conferees cannot agree to alter aspects of the bills already in agreement. Second, the conference report cannot include topics appearing in neither bill. Thus, if neither bill prohibits the use of funds for abortion counseling, the conference report may not include language to this effect. Finally, topics on which there is disagreement in the two bills must be resolved as a "compromise" between the two versions—it must fall within the scope of the differences. If H appropriates a specific amount for subsidies to cotton farmers, for example, and S appropriates a larger sum, then C must appropriate no less than the House amount nor any more than the Senate amount.

The meaning of the scope-of-the-differences rule governing conference reports is not always straightforward. The main difficulty occurs when the bills of the two chambers take altogether different approaches to a policy. A frequent way in which this happens is after the House passes a bill. In the Senate, a motion may be offered called an "amendment in the nature of a substitute." It is moved that all language in the House bill after the enacting clause ("Be it enacted that . . .") be struck and the text of a Senate bill be substituted in its place. We now have two bills with the same title ("The 2017 Control of Greenhouse Gases Act"), same House number (HR xxxx), and same enacting clause, followed by entirely different content. Especially troublesome is the circumstance in which the different content reflects entirely different approaches to the issue at hand. The House bill, for example, might empower the Environmental Protection Agency (EPA) to regulate greenhouse gas emissions, whereas the Senate bill calls for the implementation of a carbon tax overseen by the Department of the Treasury to reduce emissions dangerous to the environment. What exactly is the scope of the differences in this case, and what would a compromise look like?

Thus, the scope-of-the-differences rule requires enforcement but also sometimes interpretation. On some occasions, conferees may include a new item in the conference report that appeared in neither bill—something that unambiguously violates scope. On other occasions, conferees may compromise two disparate approaches by the two chambers in a manner that requires judgment about whether the scope restriction has been met or not—for example, the control of greenhouse gases employing a mix of EPA regulatory action and Treasury taxes.

In either situation, the rules in each chamber provide an enforcement mechanism. A member may rise to object to the conference report, claiming that proper order (as prescribed in the scope rule in each chamber) has not been observed. If such a motion is sustained by a majority, then the entire conference report is defeated. The chamber to act first on the conference report has the option of returning it to conference, where conferees have the opportunity to fix the violation. If a point of order is sustained by the second-acting chamber, however, the first-acting chamber having already approved the conference report, then the report is defeated. The second-acting chamber may not return the report to conference because after the first-acting chamber has acted, it dismisses its conferees; thus, there is no conference to which the second-acting chamber might transmit it.

Each chamber must determine, by majority vote, whether to approve a point-of-order objection to a scope violation. Often, however, a chamber does not even have the opportunity to make this determination because members are forbidden to raise points of order. In the House, debate of a conference report is governed by a special rule provided by the Rules Committee. This special rule, which a chamber majority must approve before taking up the conference report, may contain a provision waiving all points of order against the report. Thus, in approving the rule governing debate, a majority is forgoing the opportunity to enforce the scope rule, even when there are violations. In the Senate, any senator may offer a motion waiving points of order against a conference report with the same effect.

Despite the apparent procedural complexity just described for resolving chamber differences, I have reported only the most straightforward, stripped-down rendition of relevant procedure. There are many additional nuances and complexities with which I won't trouble the reader. Elaboration of Rule 28 on conference procedures in the House, for example, takes up eighteen pages in the *Rules of the House*. Even in my more streamlined description of procedure, however, it should be emphasized that each chamber has the means to enforce its procedures. Then again, as a practical matter, each chamber frequently avails itself of the option to short-circuit enforcement by approving in advance a procedure that waives points of order against conference reports. And even when a chamber does not short-circuit points of order altogether, a majority rarely sustains individual points when they are raised. Thus, when conferees break House Rule 28 and Senate Rule 27, the chambers are not inclined to discipline them.

A feature of this choreography of rule breaking is that the rule breakers, as part of the conference report, submit a *joint explanatory statement* that candidly catalogs all scope violations. In the Legislative Branch Appropriations Act of 2010, for example, the conference reports explanations for its line-by-line compromises that included the following:

> The conference agreement includes $45,795,000 for Library of Congress buildings and grounds, instead of $41,937,000 as proposed by the House and $40,754,000 proposed by the Senate.

Here, it simply remarks on the decision taken, making it clear that the decision violates the scope requirement but does not provide a rationale. Similarly, in the Consolidated Appropriations Act of 2008, one of the "compromises" on part of a Labor Department appropriation was expressed as follows without further explanation:

> The amended bill includes $3,608,349,000 for Training and Employment Services, instead of $3,530,530,000 as proposed by the House and $3,587,138,000 as proposed by the Senate.

These violations of scope are reported but not explained. In other appropriations cases, which I won't report here, the explanatory statement is quite comprehensive in describing where money in violation of scope will be spent (if above the scope interval) or stripped from the bill (if below the scope interval), but rarely is there an explanation of why the conference, in its wisdom, came to this conclusion.

In principle, the chairs of the respective conference delegations could be called upon by members of their chamber to explain a particular scope violation. However, rarely will the chambers devote plenary time to such details at the conclusion of a long legislative process that has culminated in interchamber compromise. As noted, conference reports tend to be granted blanket waivers against all points of order or, when this doesn't happen, individual points that do arise are tabled (defeated) without further discussion. In short, breaches in scope occur from time to time; they are reported by the transgressing conference committee in its joint explanatory statement, typically without explanation; but their violations are rarely questioned by either parent chamber—indeed, their report is normally granted a blanket waiver against scope violation objections.

The first example above involves a scope violation approximately 10 percent above the upper bound of the scope-of-the-differences interval but on an amount that is essentially rounding error in the contemporary spending context. The second example involves much larger sums but amounts to less than 2 percent in violation of the scope constraint. A casual examination of several joint explanatory statements convinces me that violations are not unusual, but when they occur, they amount only to small extravagances. One anecdote, possibly apocryphal, reports that when Bob Dole (R-KS), as chair of the Senate Appropriations Committee, led his delegation of Senate conferees on an agricultural appropriations bill, he managed to slip into the conference report a subsidy for a Kansas agribusiness that had appeared in neither chamber's version, a clear violation of scope. But again, it amounted to only a small number of millions in a bill that totaled many billions.

The conclusion I draw is that conferees, if not too greedy on appropriations measures or not too insistent on a legislative approach that dramatically departs from that of either chamber's version, are likely to escape sanction from their parent chamber. The definitions of "too greedy" and "dramatically departs" become less constraining on conferees if the legislation comes near the end of the term (where defeat means the chamber must begin from scratch in the next term) or if it is a "must pass" bill, one with significant importance to the president or a congressional majority. A failure to raise the debt limit, for example, would end the Treasury's ability to borrow and thus threaten the continuing operation of portions of the government.

What do failures to enforce the scope-of-the-differences requirement tell us about rule breaking more generally? In a sense, it suggests there are circumstances in which a rule is more a *guide* or a *suggestion* than an obligation. It enables a prospective rule breaker—in this case, the conference delegations from the two chambers—to regard the scope of the differences as sufficiently inexplicit so as to permit minor violations.

But then, why would the chambers tolerate departures from the rule? The answer, I believe, is twofold. First, an implicit cost-benefit calculation is made, weighing the benefits of permitting violations (and approving the conference report) against enforcing the rule strictly and suffering the consequences (the possible defeat of final legislation). Minor violations, on this interpretation, would not trigger rule enforcement—comparable to a policeman permitting travel at slightly more than the legal speed limit. It might be argued that if the two chambers could credibly commit to strict enforcement, then conferees would hesitate to depart from requirements in the first place. However, it strains credulity to believe a minor rules violation would trigger so draconian a response (as any parent knows in attempting to enforce rules with children). Hence, conferees extract minor advantages and so long as they do not cross a (vague) line, content themselves that their report will pass muster in each chamber on an up-or-down vote.

A second explanation lies at the heart of the division- and specialization-of-labor committee system in the two chambers. Members tend to serve on the committees most vital to their political needs—constituency interests for sure but also mundane things like serving on committees with lucrative campaign contribution possibilities. These committees, in turn, not only set the agenda for their chamber in their respective policy jurisdictions but also as noted earlier, are the pools from which conferees are drawn. At any given time, a legislator is in "there but for the grace of God go I" mode. I am willing to tolerate slight breaches in the rules for a current conference report, he or she reasons, in the robust expectation that on a bill from *my* committee in which I am a conferee that I will be accorded the same "privilege" to extract some small advantages. Indeed, I am willing to tolerate small departures from the rules in policy areas I care less about in order to enjoy the toleration of my colleagues in securing small benefits in the policy areas more central to my welfare. Allowance for small breaches in the rules is bound up with the larger committee system as part of a giant logroll among legislators. The rule is "on the books" and thus can always be enforced in a discretionary manner if violations are excessive—it is a club behind the door; otherwise, rules do no more than guide the behavior of conferees.

· 9 ·

Stealing Elections

Elections are the jewels in the democratic crown. Not only are they the mechanisms by which winners and losers are determined, but they also provide the means by which we hold incumbent officers accountable for their actions while in office. The first aspect, known as *selection*, in principle allows electorates to sort out good candidates from bad (however defined). The second aspect offers a potential solution to the problem of *moral hazard*, deterring bad behavior in office and encouraging good behavior by the after-the-fact determination of a politician's electoral fate. Just as an employee of a firm is selected in the first instance in a competitive labor market, and his or her performance is subsequently judged at contract-renewal time, politicians—"employees" of constituencies—face selection and evaluation hurdles through the electoral process.

The electoral means by which constituency-principals control their politician-agents—selection and evaluation—can be short-circuited in a variety of ways. In American elections, for example, campaign finance is a big concern. Large donations to the campaigns of politicians elevate the influence of large contributors on these very same politicians. Campaign finance affects selection, enhancing the electoral prospects of a politician sympathetic to the interests of the donor. At the same time, in reelection campaigns, cash from wealthy donors serves to insulate the incumbent politician from evaluative damage arising from his or her service of donor rather than constituency interests.

Although short-circuiting elections through the distorting effects of campaign contributions is primarily a concern in American-style elections, short-circuiting is not an exclusively American problem. Closed-list elections in parliamentary systems constitute another example. In these elections each constituency commonly elects several representatives. But voters don't select candidates directly. Parties do. Each party constructs a rank-order list of politicians, while voters cast votes for the party not for individual candidates. The total vote in a district for a party governs *how many* of the party's candidates are elected from that district, but it is the party list that determines *which* of its candidates succeed. Once a party's quota of elected legislators is determined by its share of the total vote, successful candidates are drawn in order starting at the top of the party's list until the party's quota is reached. A politician's position on the list is key. No matter how poor the quality of a candidate may be or how badly behaved she had been during her term in office, if she is high enough on the party list, her poor quality or bad performance will be insulated from voter evaluation and punishment. Voters, of course, may punish *parties* for the poor quality or behavior of their candidates, but they cannot target this punishment on precisely the politicians who deserve their wrath, especially if those politicians have managed a high placement on the party list.

Electoral arrangements, whether American-style or parliamentary, are imperfect instruments of constituency control. They are what they are and warts and all, comprise rules that provide at least some minimal amount of voter influence and control. But what happens when even the rules themselves are not followed? The most egregious violations of the rules of democratic politics involve stealing elections—transforming winners into losers and losers into winners by underhanded means . . . by breaking rules. Electoral fraud is commonplace in authoritarian regimes, where

elections are no more than showcases and public relations gimmicks. Nevertheless, elections are stolen from time to time even
in the most established democracies. In this chapter, I examine
four such instances in the electoral history of the United States.

1876 Presidential Election

If ever there were an instance of the corrupt reversal of winner and
loser, it was the 1876 presidential contest pitting New York Democratic governor Samuel J. Tilden against his Ohio Republican
counterpart Rutherford B. Hayes. After eight post-civil war years
of the Grant administration, the public was ready for a change.
It had given the Democrats control of the House at the previous
midterm election, a majority they retained (though smaller) in
1876. And the Democrats gained seven seats in the Senate, short
of a majority but a substantial gain, in the presidential election
year. On top of that, the Democratic presidential candidate had
polled a popular majority of 250,000 out of 8.4 million votes
cast. Yet Tilden fell short in the Electoral College, needing 185
electoral votes but securing only 184.

Hayes's victory, however, was achieved by fraudulent means.
The nineteen electoral votes of three southern states—Florida,
Louisiana, and South Carolina—were in dispute, and each had
feuding election officials who sent two different electoral results
to their respective state capitals for the Electoral College deliberation. Disputes in these states pitted, on one side, Republican
charges that Democrats had kept African Americans away from
the polls, thereby depriving Republicans of votes, and on the other
side, Democratic charges that bulging carpetbags of Republican
cash had bribed electoral officials in the three southern capitals,
producing fraudulent vote counts. Both election-day intimidation
of African Americans and official bribery were probably true—
elections are a contact sport. The three states were unable to
resolve these disputes, so the controversy moved to Washington.

Congress counted the electoral votes reported by each state on December 6, with the following aggregate result: Tilden 184, Hayes 165, 20 contested (the twentieth a technical disagreement over an Oregon elector that was uncontroversially resolved in favor of Hayes). But even here, the two sides disagreed on how to resolve the contested votes, each appealing to dubious self-serving constitutional arguments.

A compromise was reached in the form of an Electoral Commission that would assess the various positions and assign the contested electoral votes to one side or the other. If Tilden had won a single elector in any one of these three states, he would have become president. The commission consisted of five members of the House (three Democrats and two Republicans in that Democratic-controlled chamber), five Senators (three Republicans and two Democrats in the Republican-majority Senate), and four Supreme Court justices (evenly divided between the parties) who, in turn, would choose a fifth justice. The latter was a Republican appointee of the Grant administration. The commission voted a straight party line, with Hayes assigned the electoral votes of all three states. In order to seal the deal (I almost said *steal* the deal) by discouraging a filibuster in the Senate, southern Democrats went along with the commission verdict in exchange for a commitment from the new Republican administration to remove federal troops from the South and end Reconstruction.

James Grant (2011, 49), the biographer of Speaker Thomas Brackett Reed (who won his first election to Congress that year), observed that "to the Democratic and Republican high commands, if not to the candidates themselves, the White House was a prize eminently worth stealing. A certain amount of fraud was only to be expected in those days. . . . Neither party was above it. But the scale of the thievery alleged by Republicans in Florida, Louisiana and South Carolina far exceeded the norm—as did the scale of corruption claimed by Democrats against [the Republicans]. The consensus of scholarly opinion today holds that the Republicans perhaps gave greater offense to the law of the land than even the Democrats, though there is much to be said against each side." Either way, the presidential election of 1876 was stolen.

1879 Maine Gubernatorial Election

The theft of the presidency in 1876 left hard feelings in many places. Maine was one of them. The 1879 gubernatorial election featured a three-way race between Greenback, Democratic, and Republican candidates. In some election districts, Democrats and Greenbackers supported a common candidate on a fusion ticket. No candidate won a majority of the popular vote, a state constitutional requirement for election. So the final determination fell to the newly elected state senate. Republicans appeared to have won a majority there, allowing them to claim the state house as well.

But not so fast. In order, first, for the electoral result for the Senate to be validated, allowing the newly elected senators to be seated, the ballots in each senatorial district had to be approved by the (incumbent) governor and his executive council, who just happened to be Democrats. With 1876 clearly in mind, they set about to fiddle with the ballots. Specifically, they disqualified ballots cast in favor of a Republican candidate if the middle initial of that candidate were incorrect or omitted altogether. In some cases they forged middle initials incorrectly so that they could disqualify the ballot. Grant (2011, 119) reports, "When there were no defects, it was necessary to invent them. In the case of George H. Wakefield, Republican candidate for the Senate in the town of Berwick, for instance, they forged ballots such that an 'H' became an 'A.' So as Wakefield's votes were counted out, those of his Fusionist opponent, Ira S. Libby, were counted in." Overall, the results of fiddling with the ballots reversed Republican majorities in both chambers and cleared the way for a Fusionist governor.

Reed, a junior Republican congressman from Maine and future Speaker of the House, expressed chagrin at the thievery in his home state. To a reporter he exclaimed with hyperbole (quoted in Grant 2011, 119), "It is a performance which has no equal in the history of the Republic. It was no case of close majorities or contested precincts. There was no charge that ballot boxes had been stuffed, tissue ballots used or names forged. It was a clear, open, unblushing steal."

The Maine constitution required the governor and his executive council to submit disputed ballots for review by the state supreme court. At every turn in their review, the court condemned the reversals; Republican and Democratic justices found unanimously in favor of the Republicans. The incumbent governor ignored this finding but could not ignore a second finding by the court a few weeks later. A Republican senate was seated and immediately installed the Republican gubernatorial candidate. Electoral robbery was avoided but not because politicians played by the rules. They broke the rules but got caught.

Rhode Island Coup of 1935*

This is an amazing story, the sort of thing one might uncover in a third-world autocracy. Rhode Island had been a Republican stronghold until the early twentieth century. By the time of the Great Depression, it had turned decidedly Democratic. In the period leading up to the 1934 elections, it had become a state with a popular Democratic majority. This fact was reflected in the production of Democratic majorities in the state's lower house and occasional governorships. But its upper house was severely gerrymandered, with small towns and rural areas—Republican

---

*David Mayhew brought this case to my attention. He reports on it briefly in Mayhew (2011. 16). Excellent reports are found in the *New York Times*—"Democrats Seize Legislature Rule in Rhode Island" (January 2, 1935) and "Democratic Coup Aids Rhode Island" (January 13, 1935).

strongholds—vastly overrepresented, while Democratic strongholds in the cities of Providence, Warwick, and Woonsocket
were underrepresented. The 1934 elections were true to form.
Democratic governor Theodore Francis Green was easily re-
elected along with a 58–42 Democratic majority in the Rhode
Island House. But the Returning Board, the agency charged with
counting the ballots, reported a 22–20 Republican majority in
the Senate.

The Senate was an unusually powerful upper chamber. The
Rhode Island constitution not only granted it the normal powers
and responsibilities of a chamber in a bicameral legislature, but
the Senate also possessed powers rarely enjoyed by upper chambers elsewhere. This is how the *New York Times* (January 13, 1935)
reporter on the scene saw things:

> The Senate was the citadel, its membership so arranged by
> the Constitution as to enable the small towns to defeat the will
> of the populous cities. All nominees for State offices had to be
> confirmed by the always Republican Senate. . . . All the Senate
> had to do to fill an office was to reject the Governor's nominee,
> wait three days, and then elect its own candidate without any
> reference to the Governor. . . . Also years ago the Senate au-
> thorized itself to declare any Supreme Court judgeship vacant
> without giving any reason for its action. Not in two-thirds of
> a century had a Democrat had a seat on the Supreme bench.
> During these years Rhode Island more and more had become
> a State under the administration of commissions, and on
> these the [Democratic] party had scant representation.

In short, a statewide partisan minority had, through constitutional authority, the ability to thwart the popular majority, even
when the latter controlled the House and governorship. Through
a clever exercise of political imagination, in early January 1935,
the Democrats transformed Rhode Island politics forever. As the

New York Times reporter observed, "Never did a little group of men organize a political revolution more skillfully, keep a secret more faithfully, and carry through more completely what the majority call a coup and the Republican minority denounce as a plot."

One of the keys to their maneuver was the fact that the presiding officer in the Senate was the Democratic lieutenant governor Robert E. Quinn. Basing his action on the authority of the Senate to make a final determination of its members, he swore in all but two of those validated by the Returning Board. The elections of the latter two were challenged. On a voice vote (suspiciously not counted—a rules violation?) a special committee, whose members would be named by the lieutenant governor, was authorized to revisit the ballots in the election districts of the challenged senators. Quinn named two Democrats and one Republican to the special committee, which then overturned the determination of the Returning Board and led directly to the seating of two Democrats (who were declared victors in the recount by 10 and 26 votes, respectively). A 22–20 Republican majority had been transformed into a 22–20 Democratic majority. This was accomplished, despite a Republican walkout to deny a quorum, by arranging for a Republican senator to be subpoenaed and his attendance ensured by the presence of state troopers.

To assure the durability of the coup, the new Democratic majority exercised the extraordinary authority of the Senate, put in place decades ago by a confident Republican majority, to declare all five Supreme Court seats vacant (all Republican) and to replace the removed justices with a Democratic majority. This foreclosed a Republican option to challenge the Democratic machinations in the high court.* As Mayhew (2011, 16) summed it up, "In January

---

* Intriguingly, the new chief justice was the majority floor leader in the House who had been preparing to challenge for the Speakership. "Speaker William E. Reddy was re-elected by a vote of 59 to 41, the breach in Democratic ranks over this post having been healed by a caucus decision to elevate Representative Flynn . . . to the

1935 the Democrats seized the upper chamber in what amounted to a coup. They called in state troopers to corral a few Republicans toward a chamber quorum, rigged a recount of two senate district contests to their advantage, and, in a decision-laden fourteen minutes, packed the state supreme court with friendly new judges. . . . The state's long Republican era was over."

It is clear that rules were broken in the Rhode Island coup of 1935. The voice vote to establish the special committee to examine the challenged elections, the recount producing narrow majorities for the two Democratic candidates, and the use of coercion to maintain a quorum are all suspicious exercises of raw power. The fact that these maneuvers might have been vulnerable to legal challenge, necessitating the revamping of the high court, provided added weight to the suspicion of rule breaking. But one can nevertheless admire the brilliant and inspired mix of imagination and rule breaking by the Democrats. Breathtaking!

1960 Presidential Election

John F. Kennedy enjoyed a popular plurality of just over one hundred thousand votes out of more than sixty-eight million cast in his victory over Richard M. Nixon for the presidency in 1960. In a number of states, the electoral margin was razor thin. The historian Edmund Kallina (1985) reports that the winner in ten states was determined by ten thousand votes or fewer.* Kennedy's Electoral College margin swelled to 303–219, sufficiently large that changing the result in even the largest state would not have brought the presidency to Nixon. But this couldn't have been known in advance, so efforts to bring a state into one or the other candidate's column, by hook or by crook, was no fool's errand.

Supreme Court vacancy" (*New York Times*, January 2, 1935). This deal was sufficient to bring the current Speaker on board, a necessity for a few of the moves that required the assent of both chambers.

* Hawaii gets first prize, with Nixon winning the state by 115 votes.

The weeks following the election witnessed many charges of corruption and accusations of vote fraud, mainly from the losing candidate's camp. This is not surprising—it is the prerogative of the loser to point the finger. But five of the seven closest states did go to the Democratic ticket, and two of them—Illinois and Texas—were surrounded by suspicious circumstances. In the case of Texas, in which the Kennedy-Johnson ticket prevailed by 46,000 votes out of 2.3 million cast, vice-presidential candidate Lyndon Johnson was the senior senator there with a very well-oiled political machine rumored to have produced illegal votes for Johnson in past Senate races (Caro 1990). Illinois's canvass raised suspicions because of the infamous Cook County Democratic machine that had been producing votes out of Chicago for statewide Democratic candidates for decades.

A careful examination of the case for stealing Illinois's electoral votes for Kennedy in 1960 is found in Kallina (1985). The Kennedy-Johnson ticket prevailed in Illinois by 8,900 votes out of a total vote of 4.8 million. But aside from a few downstate locations and Cook County in the north, most counties were controlled by Republicans, who, it might be believed, aided the Nixon-Lodge ticket with their own shenanigans. Kallina (1985, 114) speculates that evidence of roughly twenty thousand illegal votes for the Democrats in Cook County might "counterbalance the gains [Nixon] almost certainly made outside of Chicago because of Republican control of the voting machinery" elsewhere in the state and "make a strong *prima facie* case for Republican claims" that Illinois was stolen from them. He offers a systematic analysis of recount data from state and local races. The evidence from Cook County suggests that in precinct after precinct, the vote was incorrectly tallied—for both candidates but definitely favoring the Democratic ticket. "Chicago election judges, for whatever reasons, displayed a singular ability to arrive at incorrect totals" (Kallina 1985, 116). But the scale of the incorrect tallies in the presidential contest was much smaller than that in the statewide election for attorney general. Kallina concludes that "although the . . . recount demonstrated an inaccurate count and a clear bias against Republican candidates, it did not bear out Republican charges that Richard Nixon had been cheated out of enough votes in Chicago to have altered the outcome of the presidential contest in Illinois. . . . In fact, the results of the . . . recount seemed to indicate that Democratic vote counters had discriminated less against Nixon than any other Republican." All politics is indeed local. Gallina's analysis suggests that, conservatively, the Cook County vote counters fraudulently increased the Kennedy-Johnson vote by about eight thousand, far short of the twenty thousand that would have confirmed Republican charges that the election was stolen.

Breaking rules by miscounting votes surely occurred—in Cook County and elsewhere in Illinois. But on the basis of at least one careful analysis, the evidence suggests this didn't give rise to a stolen election, though with plenty of evidence of rule breaking and certainly not for a lack of trying.

* * *

I have been tempted to include the presidential election of 2000 as a fifth case. Democratic candidate Al Gore polled at least five hundred thousand more votes than his Republican opponent George W. Bush out of a total canvass in excess of one hundred million votes. The Electoral College winner was determined by the result in Florida, which, after several full and partial recounts and competing courts ordering or preventing still further recounts, went to Bush by a difference of nine hundred votes out of six million cast. No doubt there was cheating and fraud, but the main action revolved around the question of whether officials misused their authority—courts, electoral boards, and the

Florida secretary of state. At the end of the day, it is difficult to determine whether an election was stolen, but it surely may be concluded that the presidency was secured by abnormal means, leaving the Democrats of 2000 feeling done in just like their brethren in 1876.

Part III
Bits and Bobs

· 10 ·
King David and Old Testament Rule Breaking

It is a bit of a challenge to identify rule breaking when the rules are inexplicit at best. Discovering exactly what the rules were in an ancient society like that of biblical Israel is thus no easy matter. It is especially so when the primary evidentiary base is something as elusive as the Hebrew bible, a work that is as much literary as it is historical. To sort out what one can conclude with any degree of confidence requires a combination of anthropological and archaeological expertise, a PhD in Bible studies, and the deductive skills of a world-class detective. Although the present author is decidedly unqualified in all of these respects, fortunately there are some scholarly resources to draw on. In this chapter, I rely heavily on these in order to make some sense of the life and times of King David.*

Along with Abraham and Moses, David is an iconic biblical figure who, three millennia after his life, is deeply embedded in Western culture and thought. He has been the subject of master artists (Rembrandt, Rubens); his sculpted figure is recognized throughout the world (Michelangelo). His popular appreciation, based mainly on Bible stories and fables we learned as children, derives from having slain the Philistine giant, Goliath. Years

---

*The literature I found useful includes Alter (1999), Kirsch (2000), McKenzie (2000), Pinsky (2005), and especially Finkelstein and Silberman (2001, 2007) and Baden (2014). I would also add the hilarious novel by Heller (1984).

later, he succeeded Saul as king of Israel, unifying the separate
provinces of Israel and Judah into the United Kingdom of Israel
and generally transforming a scattering of tribal societies into a
hereditary monarchical state with a royal and religious capital in
Jerusalem. David's story is one of a modest Bethlehem shepherd
boy, the youngest of seven sons of Jesse, who pulled himself up
by his bootstraps (er, sandal straps) to become a brave warrior;
a military attaché to King Saul; a dear friend of the king's son,
Jonathan; a romantic writer of psalms and exquisite performer
on the lyre; a notorious seducer of women (Bathsheba in particular); and ultimately, a brilliant political manipulator. He was
Horatio Alger before Horatio Alger; he was the exemplar of
bravery before the samurai or Spartans, and of military prowess
before Alexander, Hannibal, or Genghis Khan; and he proved to
possess the political acumen later exhibited by those masters of
the Senate, Henry Clay and Lyndon Johnson. He was all that and
more, or so the Bible says.

In a persuasive piece of revisionist analysis of the Bible, Baden
(2014) debunks much of the hagiography about David and paints
an altogether different picture of the man—less reverential, more
human, warts and all. David is portrayed as ambitious, an oppor-
tunist, and "a thoroughly amoral individualist." Baden expresses
a number of doubts in what he believes to be a whitewashed account in the Bible:

- Did David really write many of the psalms attributed to him?
  Baden suggests (through an analysis of Hebrew annotations)
  that many were probably written *for* him or were presented *to*
  him, not composed *by* him.
- Baden wonders how devoted David really was to his child-
  hood friend Jonathan in whose death along with his father,
  King Saul, he is alleged to have had a hand. At the time of
  their deaths, in the battle of Mt. Gilboa in the Jezreel Valley,

David was the royal bodyguard of the enemy Philistine king. He was therefore very likely to have been present at the battle and may even have been the source of strategic advice for the atypical battle plan involving a flanking attack from the north that resulted in a decisive victory for the Philistines (after years of small-scale frontal assaults from the west that had yielded very little).

- His presence at the battle where Saul died, or whether he had a direct hand in his death, is uncertain. However, just after Saul's death, David is presented with Saul's crown and sword as battle trophies. For a man who allegedly led an aborted coup against the king some years earlier (see below), doubts of his innocence in the regicide receive some support from this "coincidence."

- Indeed, these latter "facts" dispute yet another belief about David—his loyalty to Israel in general and Saul in particular. As a young military commander for Saul, king of the northern province of Israel, David is alleged to have slept with one of Saul's wives (Jonathan's mother as it turned out) in what was interpreted by contemporaries as a strong signal of leadership in an intended military coup and seizure of the crown. Upon its discovery, David was forced to flee south to his home province, Judah, where he survived for a number of years as the head of a roving gang of bandits, avoiding capture by Saul's agents. Times were tough in the wilderness for David, and failing to secure a popular base in Judah to support his fighters, he offered his services and guerrillas to the enemy of Judah and Israel—the Philistines. Becoming a successful Philistine commander, leading guerrilla raids into Judah to the east, he rose through the ranks and became a trusted military adviser in the royal court. Baden suggests these are actions more of a defector than a traitor because his loyalty to Israel and Saul was but a distant memory at the time.

- Loyalty more generally was not one of David's strong suits. After the Philistine victory over Saul, David left the service of the Philistines and returned to Hebron in Judah to build up a base. Having succeeded militarily as an agent of Philistia and returning with a much better endowment of resources and manpower than when he left the wilderness to sign on with the Philistines years earlier, he now could credibly threaten the small, at best loosely connected, towns and villages of Judah either to follow under his leadership or deal with the sharp edge of the sword. In noting that David served as king of Judah for seven years without any opposition from the regional power, the Philistines, Baden (2014) concludes that in fact he served as a Philistine vassal: "David became king of Judah through intimidation and coercion. The towns of Judah coalesced into a nation not by choice, but by force. David's reign was based not on love [for him], but on fear. And he ruled not as a Judahite, but as a servant of the Philistines."

- Supported by Abner, Saul's surviving general, the crown of the northern kingdom of Israel passed to one of Saul's younger sons, Ishbaal. Sensing weakness, David's forces in the south began raids across the border, testing the northern army's capabilities. Things did not go well for Israel and Ishbaal. Reading the handwriting on the wall, Abner defected to David (after having slept with one of Saul's former concubines still living in the royal chambers, again a signal of disloyalty to the existing regime). Abner ultimately died for his disloyalty—at the hands of David's minions—and Ishbaal essentially sued for peace by turning over his crown to David. But Ishbaal, too, was a loose end and was assassinated by some of his own soldiers. In all of these murders leading to David's coronation as king of Israel, the Bible attributes guilt not to David but to his minions or Ishbaal's officers. Yet all of them, in Baden's (2014) opinion, served David's ultimate objective: "When the opportunity . . . arises to open the way to the kingship [of Israel], David makes the most of it."

Baden reports many more such examples of David's duplicity and the whitewashing his reputation receives at the hands of biblical authors. It is as if centuries after the fact, airbrushing and sanitizing of a foundation mythology were the propagandistic purpose of the biblical writers. Baden likens it to "spin" and "framing" that contemporary political agents impose on public perceptions. Basing their argument on archaeological evidence, Finkelstein and Silberman (2001) arrive at a similar conclusion, viz., seventh century writers of the Bible produced a document glorifying David and the royal line leading to King Josiah, the contemporary ruler of Judah.

Was David a rule breaker? The ancient Middle East was replete with regime practices on a whole host of political dimensions involving succession and the powers of rulers. Thus, Saul's monarchy was held to be hereditary, and Ishbaal, as the eldest surviving son, was properly expected to secure the crown of Israel at his father's death. And indeed, he did. Practices, however, are not always abided by. Usurpers do seize control, for example, and David is a prime instance of this. Practices in the ancient world are more like loosely held expectations—"all other things equal, we do this." But all other things are not equal, and this is often effected by human agency—rule breaking. David's military advantages in Judah and Abner's defection from Israel's cause were things that were not equal. And this, in turn, provided the basis for David's successful usurpation of Saul's crown.

If the reader thinks this judgment is too harsh—that the world of interstate politics is a Hobbesian jungle, "a war of each against all"—then perhaps it is more appropriate to think of the transgressions of political actors as lawless rather than the violation of rules. David, like Shakespeare's Cassius, always had a "lean and hungry look," and like William J. Riordan's Boss Plunkitt of Tammany Hall, he "seen his opportunities and he took 'em." Even granting that might makes right in ancient times, the cumulative effect of the number of dead bodies piled up at David's feet, the number of women seized and coerced into his circle (and the number of their husbands "gone missing," like Uriah the Hittite, husband of Bathsheba), the dubious means by which he acquired property through theft, raiding, and the more conventional procurement of the spoils of war, and the aid and comfort given by David to Judah's and Israel's leading enemies border on rule breaking, if it doesn't actually cross the line.

I conclude that David was indeed a rule breaker, though this did not differentiate him much from any other politician/soldier/ clan leader of that era. I also believe that the Bible, while a potentially valid source of some historical events, mixes history and literature in unknown proportions, making it chancy to read too much truth into it.* Bible writers had their own agendas, and in the case of David, it probably was to elaborate a foundation myth for the creation of the state of Israel in ancient times—this was the motivation for their spin. And this underscores the difficulty of inferring precisely what rules governed political and social life, whether they were broken with any regularity, and who broke them. Rule breaking is more easily distinguished when the rules themselves are more clearly identified. But even when they are, as subsequent essays will demonstrate, rule breaking is not always obvious.

---

*Baden's fascinating account, it should be noted, is not uncontroversial, requiring reader leaps of faith in the author's conjectures and interpretations.

· 11 ·

Foreclosure, Bankruptcy, and Contract

When a buyer and seller agree to a deal, with the former giving the latter cash in exchange for something she values, we think of this as constituting a contractual arrangement. This is consummated in various ways—a handshake, a verbal agreement, or a written document properly witnessed, notarized, and filed at the county courthouse. Such agreements take place in the shadow of the law. There is a third party prepared to recognize and enforce the agreement as well as to help resolve disagreements that might arise under its terms. These are the rules.

When the conditions of contractual performance are violated, the party victimized has recourse to compensation or reparation to make himself whole, a process governed by the third-party enforcement institution. Thus, if the thing of value is not what the seller promised, then the buyer might seek a proper substitute or her money back. If, on the other hand, the seller is not compensated as required in the contract, then he may seek redress—a return of the thing of value, the seizure of some of the buyer's assets, or some other remedy (such as requiring the buyer to wash dishes at the restaurant if she didn't pay her bill).

Adverse economic conditions can make the requisite performance of outstanding obligations problematic. This is especially true of large capital purchases, the most prominent of which is a home or farm secured by a mortgage. Bankruptcy law may protect the borrower to some extent from having assets seized by the creditor. Likewise, foreclosure moratoria may keep a home or family farm with its "owner" and out of the hands of a bank or other creditor by forcing a renegotiation of repayment terms.

At the time of a loan, a creditor in principle may anticipate that there is some probability a state intervention will upset a negotiated repayment schedule. Yet for at least the first century in the United States, the legal environment favored strict contract enforcement. There were many attempts by states, and occasionally by the federal government, to intervene in contractual relationships between borrowers and lenders during times of economic hardship. But vigilant state courts and the US Supreme Court declared these interventions unconstitutional—as violations of the sanctity of contract (see Alston 1984).*

A superficial reading of this legal position is that it favored the creditor class, allowing its members to proceed along normal channels for redress when the conditions of a mortgage or other loan agreement were not honored by the borrower. Many farms were seized by creditors and sent to the auction block throughout this period. In the financial crisis of the first decade of the twenty-first century, many homes met a similar fate: foreclosure (Mian, Sufi, and Trebbi 2010). I claim the stand of the courts against contract infringement as favoring creditors is "superficial" because borrowers also benefit. The confident foreknowledge by creditors of contract enforcement reduces their risk and therefore increases their willingness to loan in the first place. If creditors believed that there would be legislative interventions whenever there was a recession or a bank run, they would be less inclined to lend or more likely to charge a higher interest rate to compensate them for these expected risks. Because prospective

---

* On the importance of precedent as a method by which the Supreme Court signals lower courts about constitutional policy, see Bueno de Mesquita and Stephenson (2002).

borrowers would be harmed by less available or more expensive loans, it is not at all clear that they are victimized on balance by a policy of holding firm to the sanctity of contract.

What is clear is that *unexpected* interventions by state legislatures or the US Congress to address the hardships of borrowers during times of economic crisis is another instance that can be interpreted as rule breaking. Each party enters a lending agreement in the knowledge that the world is an uncertain place in which the borrower's revenue stream may be insufficient to service his or her debt.* Credit markets are subject to this uncertainty. Throughout the nineteenth century and well into the twentieth century, to take one salient example, the world of farmers was highly volatile. In addition to credit crunches and general recessions, world and domestic prices for agricultural products fluctuated widely. In good growing seasons, the harvest was bounteous; supply exceeded demand and prices fell. In poor growing seasons, prices might rise, but there would be little for the farmer to sell. To counteract this, many small farmers sought to farm more extensively (by borrowing money to buy more farmland) or intensively (by borrowing money to buy more seed and equipment). With many in the farm economy doing this, the problem was exacerbated. At the end of the day, farmers found themselves barely above water, struggling to pay on their indebtedness no matter what, and incapable of doing this if things got really bad.

Court insistence on the inviolability of contract during this period provided electoral incentives for ambitious politicians to organize and mobilize debtors, especially in the north-central states with large, debt-burdened farm populations (see Alston

---

*A loan agreement may contain contingencies allowing for varying the repayment schedule, but this is something that the borrower and lender must negotiate in advance as part of the agreement. In many contracts and treaties, these are called *escape clauses* and govern the agreement when specified contingencies (also called "states of the world") arise.

1983). Many state legislatures in this region passed antiforeclo-
sure statutes during hard times, only to have them struck down
by courts. And there was churning among farm state legislators
in the Congress as well, though they typically lacked majorities
to pass bills there.*

In 1934, however, in the depths of the Great Depression, the
US Supreme Court sanctioned rule breaking. The Minnesota
legislature, one of twenty-five state legislatures, had passed farm
foreclosure moratorium legislation. In *Home Building and Loan
Association v. Blaisdell et al.*, the Supreme Court determined that
the Minnesota law was constitutional—that rules governing contract may indeed be broken. In allowing for foreclosure moratoriums, the court "prevented creditors, in the event of a default by
a debtor, from obtaining title to the land for a specified or court-
determined period of time" (Alston 1984, 446). In effect, the
court reversed more than a century of jurisprudence on contractual relations by permitting contracts to be violated. As quoted
by Alston (1984, 446) from the majority opinion in *Blaisdell*,
"the economic interests of the State may justify the exercise of
its continuing and dominant protective power notwithstanding
interference with contracts." The dissenting justices argued that
the whole point of the contract clause in the US Constitution was
that of "preventing legislation designed to relieve debtors *especially* in times of financial distress" (quoted in Alston 1984, 445,
emphasis in original).†

Historically, there had also been experiments with approaches to protecting debtors, whether individuals or firms,

---

* In all these cases, legislators may have known the courts would not countenance
their maneuvers but nevertheless played to their voters for position-taking reasons.
† In light of the scope and scale of the hardship during the Great Depression, especially among Midwestern farmers, the court majority may well have been moved
to chart a middle ground in order to protect the capitalist order from more extreme
measures being pushed by both the right and the left. I thank Lee Alston for bringing this point to my attention.

through bankruptcy legislation. It was mainly the states that exercised legislative authority in this realm.* However, this was not a very satisfactory arrangement, as the renowned constitutional scholar Joseph Story (1833, section 1107) noted:

> It is obvious, that if the power is exclusively vested in the States, each one will be at liberty to frame such a system of legislation upon the subject of bankruptcy and insolvency as best suits is own local interests and pursuits . . . no uniformity of systems or operations can be expected. . . . There will always be found in every State a large mass of politicians, who will deem it more safe to consult their own temporary interests and popularity, by a narrow system of preferences, than to enlarge the boundaries, so as to give to distant creditors a fair share of the fortune of a ruined debtor.

Bankruptcy laws sought to draw a protective shield around certain of a debtor's assets, like his home or farm, as well as to design procedures through which a debt contract could be restructured. However, as Story notes, the constituents of state legislators were overwhelmingly debtors; creditors often resided out of state in East Coast money centers. So legislators were more kindly disposed to debtors and less inclined to give "distant creditors" a procedure they might find satisfactory. Of course, leaning against this propensity were in-state creditors, mainly local banks.

Thus, both bankruptcy laws and foreclosure moratoriums constitute interventions by legislatures in the private agreements of individuals and firms. Legislatures, even though governed by a

---

*This is ironic inasmuch as the Constitution's enumerated powers for the *national* legislative branch places bankruptcy within its dominion. Yet the national legislature rarely addressed this issue. From time to time in the nineteenth century, national bankruptcy legislation was adopted, only to be rescinded a short time later. It was not until the twentieth century that a national regime of bankruptcy policy became permanent.

constitutional regime restricting the violation of contract, nevertheless permitted violations, and the third parties charged with enforcing rules—courts—reversed course by sanctioning these legislative interventions. Contracts could be revised or overturned altogether. When? When courts said they could. This change of course in 1934 had, and continues to have, market equilibrium consequences. When courts were vigilant in enforcing the terms of a contract, creditors would attribute very low probabilities of legislatures intervening successfully on behalf of debtors. Courts, in effect, provided a floor on this source of risk faced by creditors. This contributed to an increased pool of credit made available to prospective borrowers at a lower cost of borrowing. When this floor was removed by *Blaisdell* and other decisions by federal and state courts, creditors adjusted their behavior, shrinking the available pool of credit and raising its price (especially to classes of borrowers likely to be in a position to pressure legislators).[*]

It is not possible to conclude that the breaking of rules in this instance was necessarily a bad thing. If, for example, adverse economic circumstances were widespread in a particular county, state, or region, then creditors would not be keen to seize assets they could only resell at a steep discount. If, as Alston (1983, table 1) reports, 78 percent of South Dakota farms were foreclosed on in 1933, there would not be much of a market there for land. Unless East Coast bankers intended to farm the land themselves, they would retrieve only pennies on the dollar from foreclosure.[†] While some individual lenders might be able to cut separate deals with their borrowers on suspending or stretching out payments, it might be best for all of them (given the huge transaction costs of doing this on a case-by-case basis) to have a uniform policy imposed politically. Indeed, this is a major ratio-

---

[*] Evidence in Alston (1984) suggests that creditors rationed credit but did not raise interest rates (presumably for reputational reasons).

[†] Mian et al. (2010) demonstrate persuasively that foreclosures on homes during the 2007–9 financial crisis brought significant downward pressure on home prices.

nale for a well-considered national bankruptcy policy—borrowers get relief, lenders economize on transaction costs, and (sometimes) "distant creditors" do not suffer local discrimination. As Story (1833, section 1108) observed in favoring a national solution, "Very few persons engaged in active business will be without debtors or creditors in many States in the Union. The evil is incapable of being redressed by the States. It can be adequately redressed only by the power of the Union." But even if the solution comes from a state, and some discrimination against "distant creditors" remains, those self-same creditors may nonetheless benefit to the extent of saving on the transaction costs of individual, mortgage-by-mortgage, loan-by-loan negotiation. The world of contract sanctity, and consequent foreclosure, may be the worst of all worlds in circumstances of widespread hardship.

Our brief foray into bankruptcy and foreclosure has had the limited purpose of pointing out that rules must be enforced and, consequently, that enforcers must have the will to do so. Nineteenth-century courts vigorously enforced the sanctity-of-contract rule, and this reverberated throughout credit markets despite the unreliability of legislatures on this score. When in the depths of the Great Depression the US Supreme Court blinked, this, too, affected credit markets. With a precedent for rule breaking set, the odds of future political intervention in contractual arrangements, once small, had just gone up. And markets would impound this new fact into future contracts. Contemporaneous actions have downstream consequences. The rule of contract, once broken, stayed broken.

· 12 ·
Gimmickry

Rules may be broken in a variety of ways, sometimes blatant, other times subtle. Among the subtlest, and possibly the most opaque, are practices of governments in reporting economic data—debt, deficits, revenue, spending, and the like—known as "fiscal gimmickry" (Koen and van den Noord 2005).

Electorates like good news, deplore bad news, and reward or punish accordingly. Debt and deficits are "bad," loved only by the Keynesian economists who believe economic stimulation is healthy. Spending is "good," especially when targeted to my state or district, my age cohort, my income class or social group, but otherwise a matter of indifference at best. Taxes, of course, are almost always "bad."* The problem is that these assessments are mutually inconsistent. Popular spending without sufficient revenue means unpopular deficits and an increasing debt burden. Avoiding deficits and growing debt, on the other hand, means bringing income and outlays into alignment by reducing spending or raising revenue, either of which produces political casualties.

Some fixes to this inconsistency work in the short term, for example, selling a state-owned asset like a national rail system or airline or public utility in order to raise revenue without rais-

---

* As the old aphorism declares, "Don't tax me, don't tax thee, tax that man behind the tree."

ing taxes. However, these are one-off solutions to the problem. Privatizing a government activity, like postal service, does take spending off the books on a permanent basis. Nevertheless, there are only so many of these sales or privatization opportunities available. A government is not generally inclined to privatize the armed services, for example, or to sell naming rights to the capitol building.

The very strong political pressure to generate "good" without the accompanying "bad," despite the inconsistency this implies, often yields *gimmickry*—"fudges," "fiddles," "creative accounting," "cooking the books," "cosmetic measures," or more generally, endeavors by politicians to "beautify public finance statistics" (Alt, Lassen, and Wehner 2012, 3). Michael Jameson, in *A Practical Guide to Creative Accounting* (as cited in Dafflon and Rossi 1999, 78), observes that "creative accounting . . . consists of rule-bending and loophole-seeking." This form of moral hazard is a species of the rule-breaking genus.

Through gimmickry, a politician may solve the dilemma of reporting the good without having to confess to the accompanying bad. However, there are limits to how much of this can profit him or her. For one thing, getting caught cooking the books is an electoral sin, even if detection in an area so opaque is a low-probability event. In a democracy, calling out an incumbent politician on beautifying economic data is the job of political opponents. So the danger of being discovered is probably highest during election campaigns and in very competitive electoral circumstances, when the antennae of observers are most fine-tuned (even if these are also the circumstances in which the incentives to fiddle are high). Discovery is also heightened when the process of collecting, collating, and reporting economic data is transparent (Alt et al. 2012). Nevertheless, even when political opponents are on the prowl for data fudging, and independent monitoring (transparency) exists, politicians still succumb to the temptations of creative accounting. Budget numbers are opaque and unsexy;

it's difficult for political opponents to get much electoral traction on such fiddling.

Electoral contests provide one setting in which the distortion of economic circumstances is enticing. Incumbents portray rosy scenarios while opponents paint a bleaker picture. Another opportunity in which incentives to cook the books were strong occurred as European nations sought to meet qualification requirements for entry into the European Monetary Union (EMU). The Maastricht Treaty of 1992 imposed two convergence criteria that a European Union (EU) member-state economy must satisfy in order to participate in the common-currency eurozone: (1) its public-sector deficit must be at or below 3 percent of gross domestic product (GDP), and (2) its pubic-sector debt must not exceed 60 percent of GDP. Moreover, these criteria must be satisfied in a sustainable manner (making one-off solutions problematic).

Nevertheless, in the run-up to the launch of the euro, the landscape was dotted with dodgy one-off maneuvers to bring countries into compliance with the Maastricht criteria (Dafflon and Rossi 1999). France, for example, partially privatized France Télécom in exchange for a large settlement fee and accepting the unfunded pension liability of the firm. The fee was treated as income that reduced the current year's deficit, but the pension liability, which would not be confronted until years in the future, did not show up on the books at all. Belgium sold two hundred tons of its gold reserves in order to show a lower debt than otherwise—a one-off maneuver; it also engaged in "off balance sheet" manipulations, seeming to reduce its debt three days before the qualification date but buying it back after the qualification date had passed.

The evidence from subsequent experience points to more shenanigans. In order to *remain* in compliance once "qualified," members of the EMU systematically underreported deficits. The EU statistical agency, Eurostat, charged with monitoring member-reported economic data, produced decisions that "consistently result[ed] in the upward revision of deficit figures . . . [and found that] governments attempted to push the limits of accounting rules" (Alt et al. 2012, 11). This was partly due to considerable ambiguity over which accounting rules were in effect— there was a change in accounting standards just before the EMU commenced—with each member-state picking and choosing the rules that best served its purposes.

The stuff of gimmickry—"rule bending and loophole seeking"—may not, technically, entail breaking the rules as much as imaginatively violating their spirit. Nevertheless, the appearance of gimmicks represents a failure of rule drafters to anticipate strategic maneuvering within the rules. But it may not even represent that. It is believed, for example, that many of the gimmicks associated with satisfying EMU participation constraints—for instance, one-off sales of state-owned assets—were anticipated at the time of the Maastricht Treaty and subsequent implementation meetings of member-state finance ministers, but a blind eye was turned to them in order to get the eurozone off the ground (Dafflon and Rossi 1999). Indeed, some of the implementation policies adopted by EU finance ministers and enforcement agencies explicitly stated that a member-state "close" to compliance would be considered in compliance for purposes of qualification.

In sum, if compliance with a rule entails "interpretation," then a gimmick is imaginative compliance by *generous* interpretation— close to the boundary and self-serving.

Intelligence Agencies

BREAKING THE RULES BY
MAKING UP THEIR OWN RULES

We social scientists think of entities or individuals recruited to accomplish some task or to implement some policy as *agents*. I hire a kitchen contractor or financial adviser to do things for me that I cannot do well or do not wish to do on my own. In the public sphere, a legislature delegates jurisdictional authority to a committee, and an executive assigns responsibility for implementation to a government bureau. All of these agents—contractor, adviser, committee, bureau—are "hired guns." One way or another and to one degree or another, they are accountable to the principals who hired them. However, it is up to the principals to structure the relationship in advance and then to monitor agent performance, rewarding or punishing accordingly. That is, principals lay down the law, provide incentives, make the rules, and then *must hold their agents to account*.

There is a natural tension in principal-agent relationships. A congressional committee, for example, serves as an agenda-setting agent for its parent chamber; the House Committee on Agriculture, for example, is authorized to propose legislation to the full House on various aspects of agricultural policy. But the committee can exploit this delegated authority by proposing a bill more to its own liking than to that of the parent chamber. The parent chamber, however, possesses safeguards against this sort of abuse—namely, the power to amend, recommit to the committee, or even defeat legislation that displeases it. Indeed, in the extreme, a parent chamber can remove jurisdiction from a badly behaving committee, merge the offending committee with another committee, or even eliminate it altogether (as has happened in the US Congress from time to time). A legislative chamber may not always be able to do this—indeed, may not really *want* to do this—but the mere potential for doing so produces some discipline and accountability. More generally, an agent can anticipate revisions or sanctions from the principal for performance failure and adjust accordingly. In this way, it remains a creature of its creator.

Like the "internal" relationship just described between a legislative chamber and its committees, there is an "external" principal-agent connection between a legislature and an executive bureau. Bureaucratic performance is subject to legislative accountability. How is this accountability realized? On the one hand there are ex ante tools. A legislative body may stipulate statutory controls and insist on the observance of procedural requirements before an agency can act; examples include budgetary constraints, interim reporting requests, statutory deadlines, and conditions for notice and hearings as codified in the Administrative Procedures Act. On the other hand, ex post a legislature can monitor bureaucratic actions and subject bureaucratic agents to consequences whenever agents inappropriately exploit their authority; embarrassing oversight hearings, formal audits by legislative watchdog agencies, reassignment of policies or whole jurisdictions to other bureaus, and budget reductions come to mind as examples.

All of these tools are crude and certainly do not eliminate altogether the distortions inherent in an agency relationship. Some "agency slippage" is bound to occur as agents march to their own tune, one not always harmonized with the aims of their principals. This occurs whenever legislative authority is delegated to agents, whether to internal committees or external bureaucrats. Imagine how much more complicated is the problem of controlling agents when agent actions are *secret*. This is the challenge facing legislative oversight of intelligence agencies.

In a full-page spread under the headline "Breaking the Rules," journalist Geoff Dyer (2014) of the *Financial Times*, one of the most respected newspapers in the world, described precisely this challenge as the US Congress grappled with controlling the Central Intelligence Agency's (CIA's) secret interrogations of detainees from Afghanistan. The facts, reported as a time line in the Senate Committee on Intelligence study, *CIA Detention and Interrogation Program* (US Senate 2014), are as follows:

- Beginning in 2002, the CIA began rounding up suspected members of al-Qaeda in Afghanistan. Since the late 1980s, al-Qaeda had been identified as a global militant Islamist organization, founded by Osama bin Laden and responsible for the 9/11 attacks in New York and Washington, DC.
- Among those detained were several important al-Qaeda leaders directly associated with 9/11.
- In August of that year, the Department of Justice's (DoJ's) Office of Legal Counsel issued memoranda concluding that the CIA's proposed "enhanced interrogation techniques" did not violate prohibitions against torture. These techniques, including prolonged isolation, waterboarding, sleep denial, and exposure to extreme temperatures, were applied to Abu Zubaydah, the suspected planner of the 9/11 attacks. Later that year, another detainee died while being held and interrogated.
- In late 2003, the National Security Council reaffirmed the CIA's use of enhanced interrogation techniques. But the secretaries of state and defense were not made aware of these techniques until September, nearly a year after they had begun being used.
- Throughout 2004 and 2005, DoJ's Office of Legal Counsel issued new memoranda which continued to assert that en-

hanced techniques are not in violation of antitorture laws and policies; these techniques continued to be used by the CIA.

- In November 2005, contrary to direct orders from the White House, the CIA destroyed all videotapes of enhanced interrogation.

- In December, Congress passed the Detainee Treatment Act prohibiting enhanced interrogation. In 2006, the Supreme Court ruled in *Hamdan v. Rumsfeld* that al-Qaeda detentions by the United States must comply with the Geneva Conventions.

- Later in 2006, Congress passed the Military Commissions Act making it possible to prosecute individuals for violating the Geneva Conventions. However, in July 2007, President George W. Bush signed Executive Order 13440, once again authorizing the CIA techniques and stating that they are consistent with US policy and in compliance with its treaty obligations.

- In January 2008, the attorney general authorized a criminal investigation into the destruction of the interrogation videotapes by the CIA.

- In March, President Bush vetoed the Intelligence Authorization Act which would have limited CIA interrogations to those permitted by the *Army Field Manual*. The enhanced interrogation techniques previously employed did not meet this requirement.

- In January 2009, in one of his first acts in office, President Barack Obama issues Executive Order 13491, rescinding Executive Order 13440 and thus restricting CIA detention and interrogation practices.

- In March 2009, the Senate Select Committee on Intelligence (SSCI), by an overwhelming bipartisan majority, voted to open an investigation of the CIA's detention and interrogation program.

- The following month, President Obama announced there would be no criminal prosecutions of CIA officials who had acted in a manner consistent with previous legal memoranda issued by the DoJ. In August, the attorney general expanded the investigation into the destruction of interrogation video-tapes and included the possibility of criminal prosecutions for interrogation techniques that exceeded those permitted by previous DoJ memoranda.

- As the executive branch got more aggressive, the Republican members of the SSCI withdrew their participation from the Senate investigation, thus making it appear a more partisan undertaking.

- Beginning in early 2010, the CIA placed obstacles in the path of the SSCI investigation. A preliminary distribution of part of the SSCI study to committee senators began in October 2011 and some months later, to the executive branch for comment.

- In 2013, the CIA responded to the draft SSCI study and com-mittee leaders committed to incorporating some of this re-sponse into the final report. SSCI staff members met multiple times with CIA representatives.

- In late 2013 and early 2014, the CIA began withholding ma-terials from the SSCI staff and accusing the staff of illicitly obtaining documents. The CIA illegally searched SSCI staff computers to determine whether the staff had obtained docu-ments being withheld by the CIA.

- In July 2014, the CIA inspector general confirmed that CIA employees had inappropriately searched SSCI computers. He also confirmed that SSCI staff activities were not inappro-priate. CIA Director John Brennan apologized to the Senate committee leadership for his agency's actions.

- In December 2014, a redacted version of the Senate report was made public. Redactions had been negotiated between the committee and the White House.

This brief description of the unfolding of more than a decade's events reveals what many have regarded as an agency out of control. The CIA is nominally subject to oversight and review from the House Permanent Select Committee on Intelligence, the SSCI, and various parts of the executive branch, including the DoJ, the National Security Council, the Department of Defense, and the White House. Nevertheless, the agency managed to resist or obstruct various oversight efforts. Much happened, as a result, under the various principals' noses, and the agent was not held accountable.

There are several lessons to be gleaned from this experience:

1. Too many cooks may spoil the broth.
2. Secrecy has its benefits, but it comes at a high price.
3. Partisan cleavages complicate matters.

Let us take these up one at a time.

1. *The too-many-cooks problem.* This is a problem because different "cooks" apply different "recipes." In the present context, the legislature may lay down specific rules to incentivize and/ or constrain an agent; the executive may provide different, sometimes even incompatible, incentives; and the courts may provide an agent with still a different tune to which an agent is to march. What's an agent to do? In some cases, this is liberating for the agent as it pits its different principals against one other. This may make it difficult for any one of them to sanction the agent. In many instances, however, the agent is damned if it does and damned if it doesn't. The CIA was empowered to use enhanced interrogation techniques by DoJ memoranda and presidential executive orders on the one hand; on the other hand, it was chastised by legislators and courts, the former wanting to restrict CIA methods to those

permitted by the *Army Field Manual* while the latter insisted that its methods must comply with the Geneva Conventions. If the rules are contested, then it is not clear what it means to break them. And even when it is clear, it may not be possible to sanction an agent whose defense for breaking a rule is either that the one it broke wasn't prohibited action when it was broken or that the rule currently being broken occurs because the agent is forced to comply with some other requirement or rule. However, all of these may be phony defenses, cooked up to cover up a brazen disregard for the rules.

2. *Secrecy.* Under various degrees of secrecy, it is not possible for every relevant principal to monitor agency performance. Consider a detainee arguably subjected to enhanced interrogation techniques, but no representative of a principal can make this determination because it is done under the cloak of secrecy. The actual fact of the CIA's refusal to turn over documentation, its redaction of documents that eventually were turned over, the destruction of videotapes of interrogation sessions, and their general refusal to cooperate with SSCI staff shrouded agency activity in a cloud of uncertainty. Were CIA practices in violation of statutes, Supreme Court rulings, executive orders, DoJ memoranda, Geneva Conventions, requirements of the *Army Field Manual*—in short, was the CIA breaking the rules? We cannot know for certain. Precisely because of this, a rational agent, knowing his or her actions could not always be corroborated, is in a position to take liberties with the rules if he or she wished. And this can be done in a discriminating fashion—playing fastest and loosest with the rules imposed by principals who are most limited in their monitoring capacity.

3. *Partisan cleavages.* In the immediate post-9/11 political climate, President Bush's DoJ was extremely permissive. Its main legal adviser in the Office of Legal Counsel, John Yoo, crafted memoranda of understanding that did not recognize detainees as enemy combatants; therefore, they were not thought to be

covered by the Geneva Conventions. These memoranda also declared that enhanced interrogations were not instances of torture, and thus did not run afoul of US antitorture policies. This gave the CIA a relatively free hand to engage in enhanced interrogation techniques. As knowledge of these techniques leaked out, bipartisan legislative activity leaned against them, led by Republican senator John McCain, a Vietnam-era prisoner of war and victim of torture himself. Until, essentially, Obama's election, most of the political pushing and shoving was not out in the open, stymied by secrecy and national security issues. And even as the issue of the detainees and their treatment came out into the open, it was not subject to partisan divisiveness.

Obama, in one of his first acts in January 2009, rescinded President Bush's executive order and thus ended any authority for enhanced interrogation. A short time later, the new chair of the SSCI, Diane Feinstein of California, opened a committee study of enhanced interrogation; this move was supported by a bipartisan majority of the committee in a 14–1 vote. Thus, while the Republican Bush administration was tolerant of enhanced interrogation techniques just after 9/11, and the Democratic Obama administration opposed it some seven years later, the cleavage between the parties on this issue was quite narrow. However, it widened as Obama's DoJ aggressively pursued criminal charges—both for acts of enhanced interrogation and for the destruction of videotapes of these acts. Republican senators had initially agreed to the SSCI study but withdrew their support because in their view, the enlarged DoJ investigation was beginning to look like a partisan attempt to embarrass former president Bush.

Senate Republican withdrawal of support exacerbated attempts to uncover previously secret activity by the CIA. It gave the agency some cover as they placed obstacle after obstacle in the path of the now exclusively Democratic study by the

SSCI. Partisanship muddied the waters and made control of agents more difficult.

Multiple principals, secrecy, and partisanship hardly make the lines between principals and agents straightforward. Principals lay down the rules, but multiple rules laid down by multiple principals may not neatly complement one another. Agents operating at least partially in secret are able to exercise discretion regarding rules, following some while violating others. Ex post judgments about rules violations are compromised by partisan bickering and defensiveness. At the end of the day, it is fair to ask, "Exactly what are the rules, and when are they broken?" And if we are reduced to asking this question at the end of the day, then what questions are strategic agents asking at the *beginning* of the day? As grizzled veterans of the intelligence game, the CIA could, to some extent at least, anticipate the dysfunctionality that would grip multiple principals, divided by partisanship and hindered by secrecy. In short, they were well placed to break the rules because of dysfunctional accountability arrangements.

· 14 ·
Vigilantism

Throughout these chapters, I have only occasionally touched upon lawbreaking as rule breaking. Yet clearly, violations of criminal and civil law do constitute breaking (official) rules. While I haven't emphasized individual lawbreaking and its enforcement, sometimes the lawbreaking is community-wide. A group "taking the law into its own hands" is such an instance. Vigilantes do precisely this, sometimes to enforce rules that haven't been enforced or won't be enforced or can't be enforced otherwise, sometimes to achieve results that are not countenanced by the rules, sometimes to sustain practices that are informal and not part of the official corpus of law, and sometimes simply to terrorize a community.

Two images come to mind when thinking about vigilantism. The first is familiar from the western movies of Old Hollywood and appears in two variants. There is the *mob* outside the town jail threatening officials—the sheriff and his deputies—to release some alleged scoundrel so that justice can be meted out to him. Then there is the *posse*, a collection of citizens that organizes spontaneously to chase after bank robbers or cattle rustlers. Both operate outside the law but with a distinction.* The first operates despite the law—indeed, seeks to short-circuit the law—while the

---

*Some posses are *deputized* by the sheriff, and thus operate within the law. Other posses form spontaneously, often in the absence of official law enforcers.

second operates in the absence of law. In either case, mobs and posses tend to form on society's periphery, often quite distant from the thick institutions of society's law enforcement. They were common in nineteenth-century America in the small towns and rural areas of the west, for example, mining towns, where the closest forms of official enforcement were a circuit-riding judge or marshal or an army fort many days ride away.*

A second image of vigilantism is the shadowy organization that enforces "norms" that are extralegal, possibly illegal. The white citizens' councils and Ku Klux Klan roamed the postbellum South enforcing racial rules and often doing so in a violent manner—beatings and lynchings were common—both to punish transgressions (e.g., a black man looking at a white woman) and to perpetuate a culture of racial dominance through terror.

As one scholar put it, "Vigilantes simultaneously violate the law and yet are often concerned with enforcing or 'correcting' it. This uncomfortable relationship makes vigilantism a profoundly ambiguous concept which 'occupies an awkward borderland between law and illegality'" (Abrahams 1998, quoted in Smith 2014). Vigilantes may operate with the implicit support of official legal institutions, sometimes constructively seen as an efficient substitute for official enforcement but more often with official eyes averted.

Vigilantism may also take benign forms. In *Order without Law: How Neighbors Settle Disputes*, for example, Yale law professor Robert C. Ellickson (1991) describes how farmers and ranchers in Shasta County, California, dealt directly with those who violated norms of neighborliness rather than calling in the local sheriff. A neighbor is expected to help mend commonly shared fences or return a lost calf from a neighbor's herd that had mingled with his own. If someone fails to do so or, worse still, takes advantage

---

*There is controversy over this claim in which some scholars argue that institutions enabling peaceful cooperation were the norm on the frontier. See Anderson and Hill (2004).

of a situation, then "justice" can be swift in order to send a message about "how we do things around here." The locals feel no need for the sheriff in this case. This relatively benign form of vigilantism, of "taking the law in one's hands," is to be contrasted with the malignant terror inflicted on a community by a white citizens' council or a private militia.

As the previous examples suggest, vigilantism, whether benign or malignant, may function outside the law—that is, where law does not exist—or alongside the law, performing where the law cannot or will not. Its objectives, especially in its malignant form, are punitive, but they may also be protective. Neighborhood Watch, for example, is a local organization found in many urban areas in the United States and elsewhere whose purpose is to protect the neighborhood from unwanted disturbances, particularly from petty criminals and street-corner drug dealers. It is hardly a vigilante organization, unless and until it moves against these unwanted elements on its own initiative. At that point, it becomes a punitive rather than a protective organization, and thus becomes a rule-breaking vigilante group. Smith (2014, 24) presents an example of this from South Africa:

> On weekend nights in many parts of the country, members of the local Community Policing Forums walk the streets searching passersby. None of this is illegal and it is actively state supported. However, when such groups find a passerby carrying contraband and proceed to subject him to corporal punishment, humiliation, or assault rather than give him to the police, as some CPFs are known to do, their activities shade into vigilantism. It is the act of punishing—not protecting—that puts them in contravention of the law . . .

Vigilantism, in sum, is an interesting species of rule breaking. It operates outside the law and sometimes against the law. In this sense, it is an instance of criminal activity, a topic I have not embraced in these chapters. But because it is not quite criminal activity in the ordinary sense—a vigilante group is not a street gang or a criminal enterprise like the mafia—I offer it to the reader as an illustration of collective rule breaking in which imaginative entrepreneurs organize to pursue their purposes in the shadow of the law.

Conclusions

In the present chapter, I draw some lessons from the stories of the previous two parts. Let me be clear that the stories presented earlier are *selected*.* They may not be treated as a representative sample of the "universe" of instances of rule breaking and imagination. Nevertheless, they illustrate each of these and thus allow me to raise concerns, perhaps even doubts, about the alleged inhibiting effects of institutional practices and arrangements. Surely, institutional rules constrain and channel. But unenforced violations and imaginative stratagems afford wiggle room. Problems of collective enforcement—both feasibility and lack of will— allow rules to be bent, reinterpreted, and even explicitly broken. Disparities in familiarity with the rules themselves provide opportunities for more knowledgeable and sophisticated agents to deploy imaginative maneuvers. Here, I gather together some

---

* There are so many other stories of imagination and rule breaking I could have included: the emergence of a system of standing committees in the US House, engineered in part by its imaginative Speaker, Henry Clay; secession of the southern states from the Union in 1861 in a constitutional regime that made no provision for exit; Lincoln's suspension of habeas corpus; the admission of states to the Union, sometimes in accord with constitutional provisions, other times in violation; the biblical Jacob stealing Esau's birthright. The list goes on, and I hope some of these cases are explored. The grandest omission, one alluded to in chapter 3, is the Constitutional Convention of 1786 that "revised" the Articles of Confederation but not in compliance with the revision procedure set out in the Articles.

lessons from the stories that are intended to stimulate some re-assessment of the nature of institutions (and some admiration for political entrepreneurs).

Common knowledge. At the most basic level, there is the question of whether the content of the rules and their domain are widely known.* If the rules are imperfectly known, then how does an agent know whether he or she is in compliance with them or breaking them? That is, breaking rules may be the unintended consequence of not knowing their strictures (or, then again, the *intended* consequence of pretending not to know their strictures).† A related informational matter has to do with what transpires when compliance with rules is not self-evident. As Hadfield and Weingast (2014, 128) note, "Heterogeneous views about honorable and wrongful behavior make it difficult for diverse individuals to coordinate their retaliation against wrongful behavior."

Enforcement. Whether violating rules is accidental or intentional, there is still the issue of enforcement. The challenge of enforcing rules is perhaps the single most important thing that emerges from the stories.‡

In thinly institutionalized settings, like King David's Israel, both civil and religious authority governed in the quasi-theocratic

---

*I thank Torun Dewan for raising this question.

†Lawrence (2013) notes that after 1899, when the precedents of the US House of Representatives were published and made available to all members, the number of appeals of rulings by the presiding officer declined. This was partly due to the fact that members now understood the precedential basis for rulings and partly due to presiding officers feeling bound to rule in light of the commonly known precedents. No such decline of appeals was observed in the Senate, which had not made its precedents widely available.

‡The theme of enforcement is developed extensively in Primo's (2007) fine study of congressional budgeting rules. He attributes the failure of Congress to control deficit spending, despite a formal budget process that mandates it, to the lack of will of legislative majorities to live according to the requirements of the process.

context of ancient times. Norms and "established" practices were often insubstantial constraints on agents capable of and disposed toward defying normal practice. In a more highly institutionalized setting, such as the one in which the Central Intelligence Agency (CIA) practiced a policy of enhanced interrogation, multiple overseers produced a kaleidoscope of regulations behind a veil of redaction and secrecy. What was actually happening, which rules governed under what circumstances, and who would enforce them were anybody's guess (a condition exploited by wily agents experienced in operating in covert circumstances).

The main obstacle to enforcement, even when the rules are commonly known, is the unwillingness or inability of those responsible for enforcing the rules to hold themselves and others accountable to them.* Majorities allowed Speaker Thomas Reed in the House of Representatives and Speaker Henry Brand in the House of Commons to disobey normal legislative procedure. They have also regularly permitted conference committees in the US Congress to flout the constraints imposed on them by the rules. Likewise, the inner club of the midtwentieth-century US Senate tolerated encroachments on its seniority norm in order to avoid inflicting an early defeat on its newly installed leader. European Union (EU) officials allowed countries "close" to satisfying the requirements for entry into the monetary union to be considered in compliance, even if gimmickry were apparent. Local officials have routinely turned a blind eye to vigilante activity—in the nineteenth-century countryside of the US South and West, in urban settings around the world, and often in small communities where a reluctance to "call in the law" and a disposition to "settle things privately" prevail. In short, rules may be on the books, and they may be observed in normal times, but they are enforced more flexibly in abnormal times when nonstandard methods are

---

*Weingast (1997, 246) refers to this as a "coordination dilemma."

tolerated. Even so rule- and precedent-bound an institution as the US Supreme Court sanctioned violations of the sanctity of contract in the face of extreme hardship during the Great Depression (despite a dissenting opinion reminding the court majority that extreme hardship was precisely the circumstance in which the sanctity of contract most desperately required its support).

A distinction should be made between a failure to enforce owing to a weakness of will and one owing to inability. Majorities *could* have denied Speakers Reed and Brand their extralegal maneuvers. The same was true for those who broke Senate rules in the process of revising the threshold for closing debate, or those who violated the scope-of-the-differences requirement in conference reports. However, majorities chose not to. Sulla, Caesar, and David, on the other hand, could not be denied. It was not so much a weakness of will of enforcers as a superiority of force commanded by violators that allowed rule breaking to prevail. Put differently, if you have the arms (Sulla, Caesar, David), the votes (Reed, Brand), or the trust of the powerful (Lyndon Johnson), you are in a position to prevail despite your nonconforming conduct.

A key question remains: Under what conditions will a decisive coalition support or tolerate rule breaking? Speaker Reed had the votes in 1890; however, speakers before him, who arguably had the votes, had been forced to operate under obstructionist tactics by the opposition. Speaker Brand had the support of both major parties in 1881 when he moved against Parnell's obstructionist tactics; however, previous parties had suffered under this very same obstruction. Why, in each case, did majorities support rule breaking when they did but not before? To hazard a guess, I believe that violating rules or not involves a trade-off. Members of a potential supporting coalition have to weigh the immediate objective gained by the violation against the longer term sacrifice that may come from an erosion of support for the rules. In the US case, it meant giving not only Speaker Reed but also any future speaker expanded powers.* In the British case, it meant compromising, not only this time but potentially at future times, the commitment to respect the free exercise of speech in the Commons. The presence of trade-offs is what makes the rules sticky, in principle inspiring majorities to enforce rules and deter at least some rule breaking, even in circumstances in which they would enjoy an immediate gain. Obviously, this is not the last word on this important question.†

Gridlock. Many of the stories told earlier involve circumstances of gridlock. Gridlock is a condition in which a normally decisive coalition is blocked by its own rules (or possibly by other inclinations) from acting. A Senate majority is unable to bring a measure to a vote because it has not only empowered a minority to block this move but also restricted the majority's capacity to change this very rule. A House majority is not able to conduct business because it cannot produce the necessary quorum or deter dilatory tactics without the cooperation of the minority. A Commons majority is unable to rein in obstructionist activity by an energized minority.

In the case of the nineteenth-century US House, the majority and its leaders clearly desired a more majoritarian institution. Speaker Reed railed against antimajoritarian features of the House rules (though freely exploited them when his party was in the minority). It is my belief that had he figured out a way around these features while still abiding by the rules and precedents of the chamber, or had he managed to find some basis

---

*As it happened, in the very next election, the Democrats won control of the House and rejected the Reed Rules. Only after a period of suffering from minority obstruction (led by now-minority leader Reed) did the Democrats reluctantly reinstate the Reed Rules.

†Most of my examples describe *lack of will* of decisive actors or coalitions to enforce rules. For a treatment emphasizing *lack of means*, see Mittal and Weingast (2011).

for accommodating the minority without bringing business to a standstill, he would have done so. However, his imagination failed him. So he seized the authority to count quorums in an unprecedented manner and to deny recognition to those he believed were obstructing the flow of business, rule-breaking actions that were sustained by his majority (he had the votes) and only made officially permissible some weeks later when his majority adopted new rules for the chamber. The lesson to emphasize here is that gridlock is a condition of rules that makes it difficult or infeasible for slim majorities to act; it is a feature of rules that empowers less-than-majority blocking coalitions. It is a frustrating circumstance that presents temptations to majorities and their leaders to overreach by breaking the rules.

Gridlock manifested itself in a different form in the case of nineteenth-century Irish obstructionist activities in the House of Commons. Parliamentary arrangements in this period—whether the permanent rules (standing orders) or temporary ones (sessional rules)—granted majorities a great deal of latitude. Besides, the Irish members of Parliament (MPs) never constituted more than a small fraction of the Commons. The gridlock created by Parnell and his collaborators derived in part from the protection of speech favored by majority MPs. They were loath to compromise this minority right, and only after Parnell declared "total war" against the English did they come to the conclusion, only gradually reached by Speaker Brand, that nothing short of compromising the spirit if not the letter of the standing orders was the only way forward.

There are other instances of an association of rule breaking with gridlock in the stories:

- The peculiarities of the Senate as a continuing body rendered simple majorities ineffectual either in accomplishing things or changing the rules so that they could accomplish things. Weakening these obstacles involved dubious parliamentary tactics.

- Even after successful reforms reduced the threshold to end debate in the Senate, new methods of obstruction were invented requiring questionable antidotes.

- The politics of the first-century BCE Roman Republic were so compromised by a combination of complex rules, a myriad of blocking coalitions, and petty corruption that Sulla, after attempts to produce results through normal channels, simply marched his army into Rome and slaughtered his opposition.

All of these illustrations suggest that gridlock reduces a commitment to procedures initially put in place. However, it is also clear that the procedures themselves are part of the problem.

Petty rule breaking undermines respect for rule following. More dramatic forms of rule breaking often occur in settings in which petty rule breaking is the norm. This was certainly so in the first-century BCE Roman Republic, which consisted of complex coalitional politics with many institutional veto points. Corruption was rampant as veto players extracted rents from their official positions. As I noted in the earlier essay on this topic, the rules were frequently broken in minor ways because the rules were already broke. Institutional arrangements were dysfunctional in small ways, paving the way for spectacular violations often backed by overwhelming military or financial advantage.*

In modern times, the gimmickry tolerated by the EU made it more difficult to enforce membership requirements going forward. Majority tolerance of frequent scope-of-the-differences violations in conference reports in the US Congress has produced the now-routine practice of waiving points of order against these reports in advance. In these cases, rules operate de facto more as *guides* or *suggestions* than requirements.

---

*In a very interesting experimental study, Diekmann, Przepiorka, and Rauhut (2015) suggest that norm violation is contagious. In their study, informing subjects that other subjects are lying in group interactions encourages more widespread lying, much like the phenomenon of petty rule breaking in the Roman Republic.

Entrepreneurs and imagination. Another major theme of the stories in this volume is the amazing impact of political imagination, sometimes in the form of novel "workarounds" in the face of restrictive practices and procedures but other times as dubious ("interpretation") but clever ("envelope-pushing") maneuvering despite restrictions to the contrary.

Lyndon Johnson didn't break any formal rules when he elevated the prospects of junior Democrats in the Senate by restricting the operation of the seniority system as applied to prestige committee assignments in that body. The seniority system has never been an official rule of the House or Senate. Johnson did, however, violate "the way things are done around here." He did so, first, by calculating whose support he needed to cultivate if he were to realize grander personal aspirations on the national stage—namely, Democratic liberals from the North. Second, he took on board the minimal impact it would have on previous beneficiaries of seniority, realizing that most senior southerners were already well set with seats on powerful committees. Third, he understood that in reaching out to the disadvantaged northerners, he would not damage his informal, almost filial, relationships with senior southerners. Johnson had a deep understanding of the Senate as well as a keen psychological insight into his intimate bond with Senator Richard Russell (D-GA), leader of the Senate's inner club. He was a master at manipulating both chamber practices and affection for himself. He was an imaginative political entrepreneur.

So, in a different way, was Charles Stewart Parnell. As Dion (1997) and Redlich (1908) cited in an earlier chapter noted, Parnell led his Irish MPs in a novel way, inventing a new kind of parliamentary politics and thus magnifying the effect of his small band of champions of Irish home rule. In declaring "total war" against everything English, he provoked and tormented a parliamentary majority (whether Whig or Tory) with their own rules.

Through obstruction, he saw ways to make the majority pay for their resistance to a free Ireland and almost succeeded in securing it in his own time.

Senators James Allen (D-AL) and Robert Byrd (D-WV) were brilliant in teasing out new ways of doing things in a Senate rich in rules, norms, and precedents. Allen was a staunch defender of the South and its peculiar racial culture at a time it was under siege. One of its institutional bulwarks, the filibuster, had been reduced in its effectiveness in 1975 when Senate Rule XXII was amended to make it easier to close debate. The sixty-vote Senate, even almost a half century later, still presents serious obstacles to legislate; however, legislating had become easier, and the South was nervous. Allen saw something others had not—a loophole in Rule XXII. Even after cloture was voted, a vote on final passage of a measure could not proceed until other unfinished business—mainly amendments introduced before cloture—had been resolved. Allen and his confederates used this loophole to introduce hundreds of amendments before a cloture vote. Each had to be disposed of before a vote on final passage could be taken, and each, in turn, could be filibustered. Known as the *postcloture filibuster*, it effectively reintroduced obstruction that had seemingly been handicapped by the filibuster reform. Allen, like Johnson before him, was truly a "master of the Senate."

Several years later, another master, Robert Byrd, became Senate majority leader and was determined not to allow the obstruction invented by Allen to continue. Under a dubious interpretation of the power of the presiding officer to rule on the legitimacy of amendments, on one occasion, Byrd arranged for Vice President Walter Mondale to declare hundreds of amendments flawed and thus lacking merit (without a point of order from the floor, a violation of Senate rules). On this occasion, the postcloture filibuster was resolved in an hour, not hundreds of hours. This was a clever move but one without the sanction of rules. Byrd did, however, have the votes—the support of a coalition decisive in sustaining the rulings of the chair even if it lacked the numbers to end the filibuster in a more conventional (i.e., rule-following) manner. Imagination, the courage to break the rules, *and* the confidence he had the votes to support this are what made Byrd's stratagem so inspired.

Imagination and opaqueness of the rules. Let me next pick up on an issue raised earlier in this chapter. Knowing the rules is no mean feat. Knowing how to exploit what the rules permit is even more demanding. The essence of imagination, in my view, is not only in grasping the rules but also in identifying ways they might be used that others had not recognized. Imagination of this sort is all the more impressive when the rules themselves are opaque, a condition in highly institutionalized settings. In civic life, we hire experts—lawyers, accountants, financial advisers— precisely because they know things that the ordinary citizen does not. In the life of political institutions, experts arise who know the rules, precedents, and practices in ways ordinary politicians do not. It is precisely in contexts like these that expertise facilitates imagination and allows it to flourish.

The distinction between rule breaking and imagination. In the various stories, I have described breaking of rules and exercises of imagination—sometimes one, sometimes the other, sometimes both. Allen broke no rules in inventing the postcloture filibuster. Nor did Johnson in trimming the scope of seniority practices. Both were exercises of pure imagination. Marching armies into Rome were bold, illegal acts by Sulla and Caesar but followed straightforward military thinking. They were exercises in pure rule breaking, as are the frequent violations of the scope-of-the-differences rule in a bicameral legislature. However, in many of the other stories, there were elements of both. Rhode Island Democrats stole Senate elections imaginatively. Byrd and Mondale cleverly choreographed a procedure in violation of Senate rules to defeat postcloture filibusters. Many national politicians employed ingenious ways around the rules to qualify their countries for membership in the European Monetary Union (EMU). Imagination may or may not facilitate rule breaking. Rule breaking may be brazen or cunning. The takeaway point is that acts of rule breaking and imagination, individually or in combination, undermine the discipline imposed by institutional practices. An institution, as I suggested earlier, is a bit like a Gordian knot. The imaginative politician invents novel ways to untie it. The rule breaker slashes through it. An imaginative rule breaker devises subtler ways of cutting through its restraints.

Rule breaking and institutional change. In many of the stories, rule breaking precedes institutional change. After marching his army into Rome and clearing away the opposition, Sulla engaged in major revisions of existing Roman institutions, some of which survived his retirement from politics. Caesar did the same, transforming the Roman Republic into a vehicle for his personal aggrandizement and ultimately paving the way to an imperial regime. The violations of the standing rules by the two nineteenth-century Speakers—Brand and Reed—were followed almost immediately by revisions of the formal rules. Majority leader Byrd's defeat of postcloture filibusters was followed, with a lag, by a change in Senate rules.

Needless to say, this doesn't always happen. Sometimes everyone conveniently agrees to look the other way when a violation occurs and proceeds to get on with the business at hand. Violations of EMU qualification requirements, cases of vigilantism, even the occasional excesses of the CIA, constitute such instances of rationalization or disregard. Nevertheless, successful breaches of rules reflect something missing in existing practice, something dysfunctional in regime performance. Institutional change sometimes follows, but I suspect more frequently when what stimulates rule breaking or imaginative workarounds is persistent or especially consequential.

Rule breaking and welfare. I have left for last an enormously important issue, namely the matter of judging rule breaking.* Is it always bad? Does rule breaking diminish the welfare of the group or society whose rules are violated? Many of the stories in the earlier parts of the book make it evident that breaking rules can certainly have horrible effects, whether in first-century BCE Rome or twenty-first-century Guantánamo. However, the actions of the two nineteenth-century Speakers—Brand and Reed—make it equally evident that the general welfare is sometimes served by violating rules in order to save an institution from itself.

Put differently, the rules of the game that emerge from a primal environment must adapt to changes in that environment or possibly fail. Some bodies of rules possess self-correcting features that allow for institutional revision necessitated by environmental shocks. Others have more rigid requirements, for example, no method for revision or hard-to-implement ones, in which case existential threats must often be dealt with by violating rules or not at all; the Articles of Confederation was just such a body of rules. Whether rule breaking is a good thing or a bad thing, then, depends upon one's assessment of the institution that is being preserved or altered. Calvert (1995b, 262n14) notes, as a general proposition, that "viewing institutions as equilibria carries no normative or welfare implications whatsoever." The same may be said of rule breaking.

One thing seems clear to me. Judgments about responses to existential threats aside, persistent violation of rules jeopardizes not only the particular rules being violated but also the *concept* of collective self-regulation by rules. Rules emerge from primal environments presumably because they serve useful purposes for decisive individuals, coalitions, or possibly whole societies. Decline in respect for them, and the frequent transgressions that accompany this decline, undermine their normative authority

---

*I have learned much about this issue from Hadfield and Weingast (2012, 2014), Mittal and Weingast (2011), and extensive discussions with Barry Weingast.

over one's behavior as well as his or her beliefs that others will be rule abiding. This, in turn, risks a self-fulfilling downward spiral.

* * *

The stories of this book only hint at the lessons on which I have just reported. They suggest, however, that institutions should not be taken at face value or as exogenously fixed. They are more like a firm piece of putty. Most of the time, for most politicians, it is what it is and serves to channel institutional behavior. Some of the time, in the hands of a creative or ambitious politician, the putty may be molded into novel shapes not otherwise foreseen. Even the imaginative select, however, are limited to the materials at hand. The bottom line, the takeaway point of this collection of stories, is that the institutional status quo is the default option—the default option unless a politician is imaginative or breaks away from it altogether.

References

Abrahams, Ray. *Vigilant Citizens: Vigilantism and the State*. Cambridge, UK: Polity Press, 1998.

Acemoglu, Daron, and James Robinson. *Economic Origins of Dictatorship and Democracy*. Cambridge, UK: Cambridge University Press, 2006.

Ackerman, Bruce. *We the People, Volume I: Foundations*. Cambridge, MA: Harvard University Press, 1991.

Aghion, Philippe, Alberto Alesina, and Francesco Trebbi. "Endogenous Political Institutions." *Quarterly Journal of Economics* 112 (2004): 565-611.

Aldrich, John H. *Why Parties?* Chicago: University of Chicago Press, 1995.

———. *Why Parties? A Second Look*. Chicago: University of Chicago Press, 2011.

Alston, Lee J. "Farm Foreclosures in the United States during the Interwar Period." *Journal of Economic History* 43 (1983): 885-903.

———. "Farm Foreclosure Moratorium Legislation: A Lesson from the Past." *American Economic Review* 74 (1984): 445-57.

Alston, Lee J., Edwyna Harris, and Bernardo Mueller. "The Development of Property Rights on Frontiers: Endowments, Norms, and Politics." *The Journal of Economic History* 72 (2012): 741-70.

Alt, James, David Dreyer Lassen, and Joachim Wehner. "Moral Hazard in an Economic Union: Politics, Economics, and Fiscal Gimmickry in Europe." Weatherhead Working Paper Series 12-0001, Harvard University, Cambridge, MA, 2012.

Alter, Robert. *The David Story*. New York: Norton, 1999.

Anderson, Terry Lee, and Peter Jensen Hill. *The Not So Wild, Wild West.* Stanford, CA: Stanford University Press, 2004.

Baden, Joel. *The Historical David: The Real Life of an Invented Hero.* New York: Harper-Collins, 2014.

Bates, Robert. "The New Institutionalism." In *Institutions, Property Rights, and Economic Growth,* edited by Sebastian Galiani and Itai Sened, 50–66. New York: Cambridge University Press, 2014.

Binder, Sarah, and Steven S. Smith. *Politics or Principle? Filibustering in the U.S. Senate.* Washington, DC: Brookings Institution Press, 1997.

Bruhl, Aaron-Andrew P. "Burying the 'Continuing Body' Theory of the Senate." *Iowa Law Review* 95 (2010): 1401–65.

Buchanan, James, and Gordon Tullock. *The Calculus of Consent.* Ann Arbor: University of Michigan Press, 1962.

Bueno de Mesquita, Ethan, and Matthew Stephenson. "Informative Precedent and Intrajudicial Communication." *American Political Science Review* 96 (2002): 755–66.

Calvert, Randall. "Communication in Institutions: Efficiency in a Repeated Prisoner's Dilemma with Hidden Information." In *Political Economy: Institutions, Competition, and Representation,* edited by William A. Barnett, Melvin J. Hinich, and Norman J. Schofield, 197–223. New York: Cambridge University Press, 1993.

———. "Rational Actors, Equilibrium, and Social Institutions." In *Explaining Social Institutions,* edited by Jack Knight and Itai Sened, 57–95. Ann Arbor: University of Michigan Press, 1995a.

———. "The Rational Choice Theory of Social Institutions: Cooperation, Coordination, and Communication." In *Modern Political Economy: Old Topics, New Directions,* edited by Jeffrey S. Banks and Eric A. Hanushek, 216–69. New York: Cambridge University Press, 1995b.

Caro, Robert. *The Years of Lyndon Johnson: Master of the Senate.* New York: Knopf, 2002.

———. *The Years of Lyndon Johnson: Means of Ascent.* New York: Knopf, 1990.

Chafetz, Josh. "The Unconstitutionality of the Filibuster." *Connecticut Law Review* 43 (2011): 1003–40.

Cox, Gary W. *The Efficient Secret: The Cabinet and the Development of Political Parties in Victorian England.* Cambridge, UK: Cambridge University Press, 1987.

Cox, Gary W., and Mathew D. McCubbins. *Legislative Leviathan: Party Government in the House.* Berkeley: University of California Press, 1993.

Crawford, Sue E., and Elinor Ostrom. "A Grammar of Institutions." *American Political Science Review* 89 (1995): 582–600.

Dafflon, B., and S. Rossi. "Public Accounting Fudges towards EMU: A First Empirical Survey and Some Public Choice Considerations." *Public Choice* 101 (1999): 59–84.

Diekmann, Andreas, Wojtek Przepiorka, and Heiko Rauhut. "Lifting the Veil of Ignorance: An Experiment on the Contagiousness of Norm Violations." *Rationality and Society* 27 (2015): 309–33.

Dion, Douglas. *Turning the Legislative Thumbscrew: Minority Rights and Procedural Change in Legislative Politics.* Ann Arbor: University of Michigan Press, 1997.

Downs, Anthony. *An Economic Theory of Democracy.* New York: Harper & Row, 1957.

Dyer, Geoff. "Breaking the Rules." *Financial Times,* December 10, 2014.

Eguia, Jon X., and Kenneth A. Shepsle. "Legislative Bargaining with Endogenous Rules." *Journal of Politics* 77 (2015): 1076–88.

Ellickson, Robert C. *Order without Law: How Neighbors Settle Disputes.* Cambridge, MA: Harvard University Press, 1991.

Ferejohn, John. "Two Views of the City: Republicanism and Law." In *Republican Democracy: Liberty, Law, and Politics,* edited by Andreas Niederberger and Philipp Schink, 128–53. Edinburgh, UK: Edinburgh University Press, 2013.

Ferejohn, John, and Pasquale Pasquino. "The Law of the Exception: A Typology of Emergency Powers." *International Journal of Constitutional Law* 2 (2004): 210–35.

Fernandez, Raquel, and Dani Rodrik. "Resistance to Reform: Status Quo Bias in the Presence of Individual-Specific Uncertainty." *American Economic Review* 81 (1991): 1146–55.

Finkelstein, Israel, and Neil Asher Silberman, *The Bible Unearthed: Archaeology's New Vision of Ancient Israel and the Origins of Its Sacred Texts.* New York: Free Press, 2001.

———. *David and Solomon.* New York: Free Press, 2007.

Gailmard, Sean, and John W. Patty. *Learning while Governing: Expertise and Accountability in the Executive Branch.* Chicago: University of Chicago Press, 2013.

Gold, Martin. *Senate Procedure and Practice*. New York: Rowman & Littlefield, 2008.

Gold, Martin, and Dimple Gupta. "The Constitutional Option to Change Senate Rules and Procedures: A Majoritarian Means to Overcome the Filibuster." *Harvard Journal of Law and Public Policy* 28 (2004): 205–72.

Grant, James. *Mr. Speaker! The Life and Times of Thomas B. Reed the Man Who Broke the Filibuster*. New York: Simon & Schuster, 2011.

Greif, Avner. *Institutions and the Path to the Modern Economy*. New York: Cambridge University Press, 2006.

Hadfield, Gillian K., and Barry R. Weingast. "Constitutions and Co-ordinating Devices." In *Institutions, Property Rights, and Economic Growth*, edited by Sebastian Galiani and Itai Sened, 121–51. New York: Cambridge University Press, 2014.

———. "What Is Law? A Coordination Model of the Characteristics of the Legal Order." *Journal of Legal Analysis* 4 (2012): 471–514.

Harstad, Bard, and Jakob Svensson. "Bribes, Lobbying, and Development." *American Political Science Review* 105 (2011): 46–63.

Heller, Joseph. *God Knows*. New York: Simon & Schuster, 1984.

Hinds, Asher. *Parliamentary Precedents of the House of Representatives of the United States*. Washington, DC: Government Printing Office, 1899.

Hurwicz, Leonid. "But Who Will Guard the Guardians?" *American Economic Review* 98 (2008): 577–85.

Jameson, Michael. *A Practical Guide to Creative Accounting*. London: Kogan Page, 1988.

Kallina, Edmund. "Was the 1960 Presidential Election Stolen? The Case of Illinois." *Presidential Studies Quarterly* 15 (1985): 113–18.

Kirsch, Jonathan. *King David: The Real Life of the Man Who Ruled Israel*. New York: Ballantine Books, 2000.

Koen, V., and P. van den Noord. "Fiscal Gimmickry in Europe: One-Off Measures and Creative Accounting." OECD Economics Department Working Paper 417, Paris, 2005.

Koger, Gregory. "Filibustering and Majority Rule in the Senate: The Contest over Judicial Nominations, 2003–2005." In *Why Not Parties?*, edited by Nathan Monroe, David Rohde, and Jason Roberts, 159–77. Chicago: University of Chicago Press, 2008.

———. *Filibustering: A Political History of Obstruction in the House and Senate*. Chicago: University of Chicago Press, 2010.

———. "The Majoritarian Senate: Rule Interpretation and Institutional Change." Paper presented at the Annual Meeting of the American Political Science Association, Philadelphia, 2003.

Krehbiel, Keith. *Information and Legislative Organization*. Ann Arbor: University of Michigan Press, 1991.

Laver, Michael, and Kenneth Shepsle. *Making and Breaking Governments*. New York: Cambridge University Press, 1996.

Lawrence, Eric D. "The Publication of Precedents and Its Effect on Legislative Behavior." *Legislative Studies Quarterly* 38 (2013): 31–58.

Levinson, Daryl J. "Parchment and Politics: The Positive Puzzle of Constitutional Commitment." *Harvard Law Review* 124 (2011): 657–746.

Lintott, Andrew. *The Constitution of the Roman Republic*. New York: Oxford University Press, 1999.

Lizzeri, Alessandro, and Nicola Persico. "Why Did the Elites Extend the Suffrage? Democracy and the Scope of Government, with an Application to Britain's 'Age of Reform.'" *Quarterly Journal of Economics* 119 (2004): 707–65.

Loveman, B. *The Constitutions of Tyranny: Regimes of Exception in Spanish America*. Pittsburgh, PA: University of Pittsburgh Press, 1993.

Mantzavanos, C., Douglass C. North, and S. Shariq. "Learning, Institutions, and Economic Performance." *Perspectives on Politics* 2 (2004): 75–84.

Matthews, Donald R. *U.S. Senators and Their World*. New York: Vintage Books, 1960.

Mayhew, David. "'Legislative Obstruction,' Review Essay of Gregory Koger, *Filibustering* (2010)." *Perspectives on Politics* 8 (2010): 1145–54.

———. *Partisan Balance: Why Political Parties Don't Kill the U.S. Constitutional System*. Princeton, NJ: Princeton University Press, 2011.

———. "Supermajority Rule in the Senate." *PS: Political Science and Politics* 39 (2003): 31–36.

McKenzie, Steven L. *King David: A Biography*. Oxford, UK: Oxford University Press, 2000.

McLean, Iain. *Rational Choice and British Politics: An Analysis of Rhetoric and Manipulation from Peel to Blair*. Oxford, UK: Oxford University Press, 2001.

Mian, Atif, Amir Sufi, and Francesco Trebbi. "The Political Economy of the US Mortgage Default Crisis." *American Economic Review* 100 (2010): 1967–98.

Mittal, Sonia, and Barry R. Weingast. "Self-Enforcing Constitutions: With an Application to Democratic Stability in America's First Century." *Journal of Law, Economics & Organizations* 29 (2011): 278–302.

Mokyr, Joel. "Culture, Institutions, and Modern Growth." In *Institutions, Property Rights, and Economic Growth*, edited by Sebastian Galiani and Itai Sened, 151–92. New York: Cambridge University Press, 2014.

Munger, Michael C. "Endless Forms Most Beautiful and Most Wonderful: Elinor Ostrom and the Diversity of Institutions." *Public Choice* 143 (2010): 263–68.

Nippel, Wilfried. *Public Order in Ancient Rome*. New York: Cambridge University Press, 1995.

North, Douglass A. *Institutions, Institutional Change and Economic Performance*. New York: Cambridge University Press, 1990.

Olson, Mancur. *The Logic of Collective Action*. Cambridge, MA: Harvard University Press, 1965.

Pinsky, Robert. *The Life of David*. New York: Schocken Books, 2005.

Posner, Eric. "The Constitution of the Roman Republic." John M. Olin Law & Economics Working Paper No. 540 (2d Series), School of Law, University of Chicago, 2010.

Primo, David M. *Rules and Restraint: Government Spending and the Design of Institutions*. Chicago: University of Chicago Press, 2007.

Redlich, Josef. *The Procedure of the House of Commons: A Study of Its History and Present Form. 3 vols*. London: Constable, 1908.

Riker, William H. *The Art of Political Manipulation*. New Haven, CT: Yale University Press, 1986.

———. "Implications from the Disequilibrium of Majority Rule for the Study of Institutions." *American Political Science Review* 74 (1980): 432–46.

———. *The Theory of Political Coalitions*. New Haven, CT: Yale University Press, 1962.

Rowe, Nicholas. *Rules and Institutions*. Ann Arbor: University of Michigan Press, 1989.

Schelling, Thomas C. *The Strategy of Conflict*. Cambridge, MA: Harvard University Press, 1960.

Schickler, Eric. "The U.S. Senate in the Mid Twentieth Century." In *The U.S. Senate: From Deliberation to Dysfunction*, edited by Burdett Loomis, 11-26. Washington, DC: CQ Press, 2012.

Schotter, Andrew A. *The Economic Theory of Social Institutions*. New York: Cambridge University Press, 1981.

Shepsle, Kenneth A. "Institutional Arrangements and Equilibrium in Multidimensional Voting Models." *American Journal of Political Science* 23 (1979): 23-57.

———. "Institutional Equilibrium and Equilibrium Institutions." In *Political Science: The Science of Politics*, edited by Herbert F. Weisberg, 51-82. New York: Agathon, 1986.

———. "Old Questions and New Answers about Institutions: The Riker Objection Revisited." In *The Oxford Handbook of Political Economy*, edited by Barry R. Weingast and Donald A. Wittman, 1031-50. New York: Oxford University Press, 2006a.

———. "Rational Choice Institutionalism." In *The Oxford Handbook of Political Institutions*, edited by R. A. W. Rhodes, Sarah A. Binder, and Bert A. Rockman, 23-39. New York: Oxford University Press, 2006b.

———. "The Rules of the Game: What Rules? Which Game?" In *Institutions, Property Rights and Economic Growth: The Legacy of Douglass North*, edited by Sebastian Galiani and Itai Sened, 66-84. New York: Cambridge University Press, 2014.

Shepsle, Kenneth A., and Barry R. Weingast. "The Institutional Foundations of Committee Power." *American Political Science Review* 81 (1987): 85-105.

———. "Structure-Induced Equilibrium and Legislative Choice." *Public Choice* 37 (1981): 503-19.

———. "When Do Rules of Procedure Matter?" *Journal of Politics* 46 (1984): 206-21.

Simon, Herbert. *Models of Man*. New York: Wiley, 1957.

Smith, Nicolas Rush. "Conceptualizing Vigilantism: Possibilities for Political Science." Paper presented at the Annual Meeting of the American Political Science Association, Washington, DC, 2014.

Story, Joseph. *Commentaries on the Constitution of the United States*. 3 vols. Boston: Hilliard-Gray, 1833.

Stouffer, Samuel. *The American Soldier*. Princeton, NJ: Princeton University Press, 1949.

Strahan, Randall. *Leading Representatives: The Agency of Leaders in the Politics of the U.S. House*. Baltimore: Johns Hopkins University Press, 2007.

US Senate. "CIA Detention and Interrogation Program." *Washington Post*, December 2014. Retrieved August 31, 2015 (http://www .washingtonpost.com/wp-srv/special/national/cia-interrogation -report/document/).

Wawro, Gregory, and Eric Schickler. *Filibuster: Obstruction and Lawmaking in the United States Senate*. Princeton, NJ: Princeton University Press, 2006.

Weingast, Barry R. "The Political Foundations of Democracy and the Rule of Law." *American Political Science Review* 91 (1997): 245–63.

Index

www.ingramcontent.com/pod-product-compliance
Lightning Source LLC
Chambersburg PA
CBHW032145020426
42334CB00016B/1226